The Angler's Chest

By Don Tucker

Printed in Victoria, BC, Canada.

ISBN: 978-1-4269-2484-2 (sc)

*Our mission is to efficiently provide the world's finest, most comprehensive book publishing
service, enabling every author to experience success. To find out how to publish your book, your
way, and have it available worldwide, visit us online at www.trafford.com*

Trafford rev. 1/27/2010

 www.trafford.com

North America & international
toll-free: 1 888 232 4444 (USA & Canada)
phone: 250 383 6864 ✦ fax: 812 355 4082

Dedication

This book is dedicated to the "Lady" who made so many of those trips to field and stream even more enjoyable. The "Lady" who made the hot dogs, baked the cakes, washed and dried the muddy overalls, and sat up late at night, waiting and worrying about me.

Thanks, Mom!!!!!

Contents

Chapter One

....

The Journal

Fishing for me has always been an important part of what makes life worth living. To me it is the perfect sport. There are so many kinds of fish, with even more ways to catch them. There's an angle for every for every angle. All you need is water and the ability to think big! I believe, if those folks in the Middle East where it is so dry, had several ponds and a lake or two to fish in, maybe they wouldn't have time to fight and kill each other.

Terry Joe Aultman took me with him in the summer of 1963, when I was only six years old, and I fell in love with the feel of a tug on my line. Fishing floats my troubles away, renews my spirit, and fills my heart with joy. Fishing is not a contest against the fish, but a contest with nature and discovering its' special wonders. It is for all ages, young and old.

My "Ol Journal" has many accounts of hunting and fishing trips with "my boys", (family members, sons of friends, and youngsters from church). Fishing is for all ages, young and old. One of my warmest memories is a youngster's grin seeming to wrap around his whole head as he held up his first fish. To a kid, every caught fish is a trophy. I have been showing kids the wonders of the great outdoors for many years.

Two of these boys, Corey Farris and Kevin Eads, grew up and became United States Marines. While at Paris Island for basic training, the "tough as nails" sergeant had them wading through a swamp with a fifty pound pack on their backs. The sergeant came up to Kevin and said, "How do you like this, Alabama?" Kevin replied, "nothing to it, sir." The sergeant asked, "You mean you've done this before?" Kevin's answer was, "Yes sir, but in the dark."

In March of 1972, I started putting the facts of each trip to a field or stream down in writing. I had read of a man who recorded all his hunting and fishing trips because it would improve his luck by rereading the facts and jogging his memory. I was inspired to do the same, and began recording the facts on each month's calendar. Most of the information listed the date, wind direction, water condition, who was with me, and of course, the place. By doing this, I did indeed improve my luck.

As all those calendars began to add up, I realized that I needed one book with space enough to record the stories that went along with the trips. While every trip might not have a good story, that did not diminish its true worth as a golden memory. Each memory will be cherished as the years go by.

The book I chose to be my journal was a big green ledger book. I went to the book store without a clue as to what kind of book I needed, but when I saw that green ledger book I knew I had found the perfect book for logging all my hunting and fishing adventures. It brought back memories of my dad at the service station he owned. When I was about eight years old I heard him talking to a customer about "getting credit". I liked the idea of buying something and paying it off later.

I asked Mom to arrange credit for me at the big J.A, Kelly General Store here in Eldridge. By Wal-Mart standards, the Kelly store was very small, but to me it was an awesome place filled with anything you could want. There were two levels to the store. The upper one for foods and the lower for "dry goods" and hardware.

The main attraction for any kid was the beautiful, oak and curved glass candy counter filled with a huge assortment of penny and nickel candy. So many colors and flavors. How could a little guy choose? My favorite was a cherry flavored piece of rock candy and when I was really careful I could make it last almost an hour. After the candy counter came the grocery section and the meat department. A fresh slice of "baloney" and some cheese, with some crackers from the cracker barrel, made a real working man's banquet.

As you started down the eight to ten steps you saw a large tank on your right. It held kerosene and had a handle on it for pumping the kerosene into the buyer's container. Oil lamp's lit many homes with oil from that tank. When you reached the bottom of the steps, more glass cases held pocket watches, jewelry, and assorted items. Then there were dresses, shirts, ""yard-goods", thread, sewing notions, stacks of Liberty overalls and assorted items.

In the middle of the building you could find overalls, work-clothes, and toys when Christmas was near. The back wall held work boots, Sunday slippers, and school shoes for the kids when summer ended. There was a building at the side, between the store and Opal and "Poocher's" Cafe, that held feed, grain, and other things a farmer might need. The whole store was filled with wonderful smells, oranges, apples, bananas, leather, spices, and the oiled oak floors.

The front steps were the weekend gathering place of the town drunks and was avoided by all "respectable" people. These drunks were much like Otis Campbell of the Andy Griffith show and never seemed to cause any real problems to anyone but themselves.

This store was the center of our little town and it was made very special by the four men who managed it. They were the Kelly brothers, Howard, Lawton, and Gaston, and Clovis Fikes, who worked for them for many years. They were real southern gentlemen, always courteous, kind, and helpful to anyone who entered their store. Each customer was welcomed, regardless of age, size, or financial status and when I arrived, looking for "credit", they gave me the "Grand Tour". Finally they asked what I needed and I said I needed a nickel's worth of B B's. The BB's were bagged and I was escorted to the side room where a big roll-topped desk was opened. A big green ledger was taken out and my purchase was entered. That was the second most impressive book I had ever seen. The first was the Bible.

I paid off the debt three days later and continued to do business with the Kelly's until the store closed. The old store building was recently torn down and all that remains is a vacant lot. The Kelly brothers are all gone now and are buried at the Tucker Cemetery, just south of Eldridge. As caretaker of the cemetery it always brings a smile to my face when I remember that nickel's worth of BB's and "gettin' credit".

My journal occupies a place of honor on top of my angler's chest. Each entry tells the story of this angler's love affair with the great outdoors.

Chapter Two

Crickets

Have you ever gone fishing with just a cane pole, a good friend, and a box of crickets?   Folks try to over complicate things. The simple pleasures of life are always the best. I remember a few years ago I loaded up my twelve foot aluminum boat with kids, cane poles, a cooler of drinks and hot dogs, and great hopes for a trip down the Sipsey River. My friend Scott Henderson, his seven year old son, Chad, Chad's buddies, Zack Tucker, and Tyson Lawrence made a full crew. The boy's were small enough to stand in the boat without falling overboard. I slowly paddled the boat up close to every stump and log and each one yielded a few fat bream. As soon as one was hooked, my pint sized fishermen would say, "Worm me" or "Take this one off", or "Wow, look at this one". I have never worked so hard, but never any more fun. Those kids grinned all the way around their heads every time a trophy fish was boated. That's what is so great about kids; size does not matter to them. If that fish is just three inches long, he's still worth grinning about.

The Hendrix family is rich in light hearted stories that bring a smile to our lips and a song to our hearts. Each year we gather for a reunion at the Joe Wheeler State Park on the Tennessee River and retell the good times, and a little of the bad, of growing up, and raising families. I always bring about twenty small cane poles, fully rigged with lines, hooks, and sinkers. The dock at the lodge provides the perfect place for several kids to fish in a clean safe area. With the help of dads, uncles, cousins, and kinfolk from Michigan to Texas and everywhere in between, we give those kids the same opportunity to enjoy that same wonderful feeling the boys experienced in that twelve foot aluminum boat years ago. They all get to catch at least one or two fish, then I pull out my camera and take pictures of those million dollar smiles.

A few years ago I decided to have an impromptu cricket race for the little fishers. A big circle was cleared and each child was given a cricket. The first cricket to exit the circle was the winner. Now some of those were well motivated to get away, but some had been held onto so tightly they never left the starting line. The next day my niece, Kara, whose son, Jacob had won a cricket race, told me of the five year old's bedtime prayer. Jacob prayed,"Thank you God for Mommy and Daddy, and thank you God for that cricket."

Another cricket tale has to do with my cousin, Kenny, from Michigan coming down for a much anticipated fishing trip down the Sipsey River. We loaded up all our supplies and I took along three hundred crickets. As we pushed off it became apparent that my boat, "The Titanic" was in much need of repair. Soon, we discovered that when water touches a cardboard box with 300 crickets in it, it is like kicking the top off of a fire ant hill. They go everywhere! Later,

Kenny said he had doubts about my boat since even the crickets were abandoning ship.

When I was growing up, catching bait was as big an adventure as going fishing. Our old pump house was cool and damp inside, and when you opened the door, the biggest crickets in the world would jump everywhere. I tried to catch them by hand, but they were just too fast. I asked Dad how to catch these super crickets but he would just laugh and say for me to figure it out. At night I would dream about catching the next world record bass using these super crickets as bait. My Granny Tucker gave me some advice one night over a game of dominoes. She said, "Son, those crickets really like potatoes, because they were always in my potato cellar. If you know where they can be found, get yourself a minnow basket and put a few 'tater peelings in it. Leave it overnight and check it the next day".

It took two five gallon buckets of returnable bottles to buy a new minnow basket from the J.A. Kelly store. That evening I put some tater peelings in my new basket and placed it in the pump house. The next morning I couldn't wait to see what I had. When I opened that door I couldn't believe my eyes. That minnow basket was full of cellar crickets! With a ready supply of bait, fishing became easier, because no fish could resist those big, plump crickets.

Several years later I was headed down to Mr. Wyman Jones' farm for some late summer wade fishing. Mr. Wyman was in his garden picking tomatoes, squash, and okra. I stopped to visit a while and noticed that his garden and yard had lots of grasshoppers. I grabbed my dip-net and began catching my fish bait. Mr. Wyman offered to hold the quart jar while I caught them. We would snatch one here and another over there. We almost had the jar full when Mrs. Jones came walking up with two big glasses of lemonade. She said, "You two come over here and sit down in the shade and cool off. I think both of you have been out in the sun too long."

I have always had success catching crickets while mowing the yard. Black crickets are easy to catch once the grass is cut. Three years ago Mom bought a new Cub Cadet lawn mower and I couldn't wait to try it out. I made a couple of trips around the yard and got ready to catch me some crickets. I finally spotted one, jumped off the mower to get him and the mower stopped running. I got back on the mower started it up, went a little farther and spotted another cricket. Without thinking, I jumped off the mower again, and the motor stopped again. I went in the house and told Mom that we had bought a lemon. She laughed and said, "It's supposed to do that. It's a safety feature, because the folks who made it didn't like to fish as much as you do".

Every time I go fishing I try to learn something new. I have fished with so many anglers over the years and learning from them gives me the confidence to fish anywhere and any time. A select few who I call the "old masters" are J.T. Tidwell, Rusty Whitehead, Roy Aldridge, and my Dad. These men could catch fish anywhere at anytime in salt water or fresh.

My journal lists many wonderful fishing adventures with the men listed above, but this one stands out in my memory. In June of 1988, Roy Aldridge, and I went float fishing on the Sipsey River. Mr. Roy was 82 years old, when we made that trip, and he was a fly-rod expert. It was a joy to watch him flip that cricket around. Mr. Roy was also an artist. He could make anything out of wood; toys, furniture, slingshots. He could bring anything to life in his hands, but he specialized in fly-rods and musical instruments. Mr. Roy gave me some advice on this trip. He said, "Son, never become so good at a hobby that it interferes with the joys of living." Every time I flip a cricket at a stump or weed bed with one of Mr. Roy's fly-rods I experience that joy of living."

Chapter Three

....

Real Red Worms

I **have discovered, in fifty** years of life on this earth that joy and happiness have nothing to do with a nine to five job, paying taxes, or the price of gas. In a country gone mad over creature comforts of all shapes and sizes, we all crave that feeling of being needed and loved. I have been blessed on many a trip to field and stream with that warm and happy feeling.

As any good fisherman knows, the quality and quantity of your bait makes a great time possible. I came to the conclusion that live bait was better than artificial as soon as I priced a sixteen foot bass boat, a two hundred dollar open faced reel, and a one hundred fifty dollar graphite rod. A cane pole cut off the river bank, a little fishing line, a hook, a cork, and some good 'ol red worms are all you really need. I might have a dollar invested in the whole rig.

Another thing all good fishermen know is that it is important to keep your bait as fresh as possible. I think this little story illustrates this pretty well. An insurance salesman had a little free time at one of his travel destinations. An avid fisherman, he would always ask the locals where the best fishing holes were located. Being told that the mill pond behind city hall offered good fishing all day long, he went to try it out. As he began to cast his brand new, three hundred dollar, rod and reel with a twelve dollar artificial bait tied on, he noticed a little boy, about 8 or 9 years old, fishing with a cane pole. The boy was dragging in fish after fish while his expensive equipment yielded only frustration. Being a salesman he knew that listening was a great learning tool, so he walked over to the little boy and asked his secret to catching all those fish. The boy mumbled, "Umphh, Umphh." The salesman asked again and again and the boy replied the same mumbled words. Finally, the salesman told the boy to take whatever he had in his mouth out. The boy unloaded a big wad of wriggling red worms and said, "You have to keep your bait fresh".

J. T. Tidwell "showing off"

One of my best fishing buddies, J.T. Tidwell, also believes in this theory of the fresher the bait the better the fishing. J.T. grows kids and cattle on his Fayette county farm. When we go fishing, the first thing we do is dig for red worms, under countless cow patties, out behind his barn. The fresher the better certainly holds true when collecting bait with Mr. Tidwell!

J.T. and I have spent many days on the bank of the Sipsey River. We always catch fish and tell story after story of good times spent "yarning" on that old river. Most trips are good ones, some are great, and precious few are pure joy. Several years ago J.T. and I went to the Whitley Bend for a day of fishing. The day was great, we had lots of bait, the weather was beautiful, the fish were biting, and we had plenty of food and drinks. (Days like that can be rare.) We were not able to keep all our lines in the water at the same time. We both were either taking fish off or putting bait on the hook. J.T. smokes Viceroys one after the other and he was trying to land a fish, bait a hook, smoke a cigarette, and tell a story all at the same time. In all the excitement, his cigarette fell out of his mouth and he never knew it was gone. He just kept on smoking that invisible cigarette and kept on talking.

Sucker fishing is another fine art that J.T. taught me. All you need is a cane pole, a cigar shaped cork, line, hook, and sinker. The bait to use is the red worm, not those worms that look like baby snakes. Now, find a creek mouth on the Sipsey River in the spring, and get set for some line stretching fun. Why anyone would want to eat these fish is a mystery to me. They taste like bass, but they are full of tiny "Y" shaped bones. In order to eat them, you must fillet each side down to the backbone, then slice them an eight of inch down and across. Then you mix a raw egg or two with the meat, wad it up, and make patties out of it. Deep fry the patties and have onions on the side, then you're ready for dinner, provided you still have enough energy left to eat.

Suckers are odd looking creatures, to say the least. Their mouth is at the bottom of their jaw, which makes it easier for them to suck up any morsel that might be on the bottom of the stream. Over the years I have introduced many young anglers to this type of fishing. Once they catch a sucker, I tell them to stick their finger in its mouth. They always look at me with suspicious eyes, but to show me they have no fear, in it goes. I guess for a youngster, sticking your finger into something wet and slimy is quite unsettling, but a great lesson is soon to be learned from it.

When we head home I always let the boys "tote" the fish. Most trips, filling a stringer is no problem. When we get home and I tell them how tired I am, they want to help clean the fish. A big fish fry is soon planned and I always bring some catfish fillets along with the sucker patties. We get all the fish cooked and they are anxious to try a new taste, but soon discover why catfish are farmed commercially, and not sucker fish. As they look for a place to spit out a mouth full of sucker, I smile and yell, "Suc-k-e-rrrrr!!!"

Chapter Four

....

Night Fishin'

With over **30,000 different kinds** of fish in the salt and fresh waters of our planet, there are almost as many ways to catch them. Most fisherman prefer daytime to pursue their favorite species because darkness has its' own hidden horrors. It's easier to get turned around and lose your way at night on a large body of water, hidden obstacles such as stumps, logs, and rocks can make night fishing a "fun outing" or a "downright" nightmare, and snakes are more active at night.

I love to fish wherever and whenever the opportunity presents itself and night fishin' offers one thing that keeps me coming back. It's so much cooler at night, and I think the fish are happier, too. Down on the Sipsey River you can "bank fish", set out hooks, or gig at night.

Folks, my age and older, who have done any giggin', all wade gig. It is mainly a spring thing to go sucker giggin', and only a few other idiots and me will gig into summertime. You would be surprised to see how fast a fellow can run "the hundred" in waist deep water when a cottonmouth is trying to get in his overalls!

The last few years I have let the boys gig out of the boat, just to kill an hour or two between checking my set hooks. They've gotten so good at it that now it is all they want to do. August 21, 1998 proves this point. Chad Henderson, his friend Tyson Lawrence, Chad's dad Scott, and myself were giggin' above the Curt Hubbert bridge. Chad and Tyson might have weighed ninety pounds each, so when Chad gigged a big gar fish, out of the boat he flew. As we loaded him and his fish back into the boat I pushed the boat off from a weed bed next to the bank. I must have poked a big bass in the tail, because the next thing we knew he landed in the boat between Scott's feet. Scott thought a big cottonmouth had loaded up, too. He let out a yell that would curl your hair. I said, "Hold on boys, you've got them surrendering".

We really got a big laugh out of the whole commotion.

Thinking about Scott and the bass reminded me of something that happened when my dad, Mr. Arlon Tucker, and his brother went fishing down in the Walker bottoms on the river. They got their lines set out and were gathering firewood when Mr. Arlon let out a yell. He hollered, "Boys, come quick. I've got a snake up my britches leg!" Mr. Arlon had a death grip on something about half way up his right thigh. Dad asked him what they could do to help. Mr. Arlon replied in all earnestness, "Cut this thing out!" So Dad cut all the way around, careful not to cut off something that Mr. Arlon might need. When he finished cutting, there instead of a scary snake was a large bullfrog and Mr. Arlon had squeezed him so tight that his insides were outside. That goes to show that folks will do things at night they would never do in the daytime.

A favorite place to go settin' out hooks is Gorman's. The water is deep, the scenery is breath taking, and the fish grow big. Once we get our hooks set out, we stop to take a break. The overhang is a big flat rock about twenty feet above the water, and the water is probably about twenty feet deep, just right for swimming. After trying every dive, somersault, and cannonball known to man, the boys get silly and one day they were jumping out into thin air and pulling their shorts down just before they hit the water. Never being one to pass up a photo opportunity, I pulled out my little camera and made some pictures. This trip was on the seventeenth of July in 2004, before "Flags of Our Fathers" came out. I had seen on the History channel where one of the flag raisers' back was to Rosenthal when he made famous picture. When the photo reached the United States, the marine's mom instantly knew her son, even though all she could see was his behind as he helped plant the flag pole. A month or so later we were having a fish fry at one of the boy's grandmother's house. I decided to see if Miles' mom could pick out her son between three bare bottoms. With absolute confidence, she correctly picked out her red faced Miles' white bottom.

Night fishing is not for the inexperienced angler. Knowing your way around is essential to fishing safety. Having good night eyes can save an angler from turning a fun trip into a nightmare. Not too long ago my cousin, Marcus and his wife Johnnie were driving home from church when their car drifted across the yellow line several times. Johnnie asked Marcus what was wrong and he said he was having trouble seeing out of his right eye and asked her to get him an appointment with his eye doctor. They went to the appointment and she anxiously waited for news. After examining Marcus, the doctor called Johnnie back and sent Marcus to the waiting room. The doctor said, "Mrs. Wyers, I didn't want to embarrass your husband, but there's nothing wrong with his right eye, the lens is missing from his glasses."

Chapter Five

··

The Hook Drawer

As every good fisherman knows, the sharper the hook, the more successful you will be. Hook manufacturers advertise their products as super sharp, weedless, or needlwpoint. Eagleclaw's very name speaks volumes about their product.

On September 9, 2008, I loaded up my pickup, Ol' Blue, and headed down to Curt Hubbert Bridge to set out hooks. Chad Henderson, Craig Roden, and Seth Cosby made up my crew. We had barely got away from the bank when Seth proclaimed that he saw something and he was claiming it as his own. There was a drift of logs and debris out in the middle of the river, and hanging off from a big limb was a shiny, deep diving, artificial lure, practically new and the hooks were not even rusty. Seth kept reminding us that he saw it first. Chad told him that sometime or other he would lay it down, and then it would be his. For the next two hours ol' Seth didn't lay that lure down, not even when we stopped to eat our hot dogs.

Seth was standing up in the boat holding a spotlight in one hand and his lure in the other when they spotted a big gar. Excitedly the boys told me to turn my trolling motor wide open. They were watching the fish instead of where we were going and we ran into a snag and suddenly came to an abrupt stop. Seth would have gone flying out of the boat if he had not put out his hand, the one holding that prize lure, to catch himself. His hand crashed into Chad's head, and now Seth was hooked into Chad's ear. All thoughts of the big fish evaporated. I paddled the boat to the bank so I could try to untangle them. Blood was running down Seth's arm and flowing down Chad's neck. I had to use my pocket knife to separate them. Craig asked me if I had any doctoring experience and I told him, "No, but I did stay at the Holiday Inn last night!"

When the Hendrix reunion rolls around, the older folks gather around to tell of old times and younger days. My uncle B.G. "Bud" Farris tells about a fishing trip down on Mallard Creek. He and his brother, Frank Jr., were trying to catch a few fish for supper, but the fishing was slow. The boys were in the 7-8 year old range, and as youngsters will do, they got bored. They started whipping their cane poles through the air. Suddenly, one very sharp hook lodged in the end of Jr.'s nose. They didn't think to use their pocket knife to cut the line, or that they could bite the line in two, so, Bud led his brother all the way home by his nose.

Last year, I was sitting in on one of the joking and story telling sessions when one of the many college age youngsters came walking by. Bud reached out and grabbed him by the arm and asked how his schooling was going. He replied that he was going for his PHD. When Uncle Bud told him that he already had his PHD he was surprised and said he didn't even know that Bud went to college. With a big grin on his face, Bud told him that his PHD stood for "Post Hole Digger".

Speaking of being hooked, some of the men in our family were hooked on driving a truck for a living. Uncle Bud was closing in on 80 years old, when he finally retired from driving. My Dad also loved trucking, and he could give you directions to anywhere. Dad trucked cross country to California in the 1950's, before interstate highways made it so much easier to travel. Dad told us how in preparing to cross the desert, they would buy large blocks of ice, place them inside the truck cab, turn the fans on, and roll the windows up. We can't imagine going anywhere without air conditioning in our cars, but back then, you had to make do.

I work at the Southeast Wood Treatment plant in Nauvoo, Alabama, and we receive, on average, a tanker load of chemicals every two days. One morning one of our regular tanker truck drivers came walking in and said, "Tucker, every time I come here, you are sitting on that counter top." I replied that they pay me think around here, because I'm too lazy to work. The driver then asked what I had been thinking about and I said that I believed that I had missed my calling. Curious, the driver then asked what I thought my calling was. I told him I should have been a truck driver because, "I have a PHD that stands for Post Hole Digger".

Chapter Six

··

Lead Sinkers

Every **good fisherman knows the** proper weight is essential to catching fish.

This is accomplished by using weighted hooks or crimping a lead weight directly onto the line. Line buoyancy, or lack of, presents the bait at the proper depth, where you hope the fish will be found. The last few years have seen the tackle shops switch from lead to steel. The idea being that lead is bad for the environment and steel is good. I think and believe that the almighty dollar is what is good for the environment. Lead sinkers and lead shot have always managed to keep me well fed. I do suppose too much of anything is bad for your health. It can also lead to a good laugh.

August 28, 1991, found me fishing the Elk River up in Tennessee. Mom wanted to visit some of her Tennessee cousins and her sister, Oveta told me that I could look forward to having a good time. I had met the cousins at one of our family reunions and they had invited me to come up and do some fishing with Mr. Leon. He told me that his property bordered on the river and he could show me where the big ones were.

After all the neck huggin' and "let me show you our cat, dogs, birds, chickens, and squirrels, Mr. Leon and I slipped off to the river. His property did border on the river, but a sixty foot bluff had to be traversed just to get down there. He was well into his sixties, and he might have fished that stream in years past, but no one had been down that bluff since Ol' Davy Crockett.

Mr. Leon kept reminding me that he was an expert fisherman, and I had better be at my best in order to beat him. When he asked me to rig up a cane pole for him, seeing how his eyesight was not what it used to be, I decided to get an edge on him. As I tied the line, hook, positioned the hook just right, I crimped a larger lead weight onto his line. It was just big enough to sink the cork and keep him busy jerking that cane pole, trying to catch that fish that was pulling his cork under all the time. After a while, I had fifteen or so keepers on the stringer. I told Mr. Leon to let me swap poles with him and see if I could catch that smart aleck fish that was giving him so much trouble. I lightened some of the excess weight from his line and put the cork back in the water. Three minutes later, a fine four pound channel catfish lay flopping on the bank. Mr. Leon was finally convinced that I was the best fisherman that he had ever seen.

Fishermen are always looking for new ideas and willing to adapt to changing water conditions. June 28, 1977, I headed for the Pierce Shoal in the upper end of Walker Bottoms to catch our supper. We planned to "bump" a few catfish. Some folks call it "noodlin", but by either name it is the same thing. All you have to do is locate a rock, hollow log, or a rock shelf where the big catfish clean out a place to lay their eggs. Catfish on the Sipsey generally go on bed in June, the last of

May, or the first of July, and if you are persistent, you'll find fish. The big ones seem to use the same spots year after year. Experience really counts here, because if you know where to look, you will probably be rewarded. All the gear you need for one of these trips is a bumping hook, a frying pan, some cooking oil, flour, salt, and some potatoes. My bumping hook is almost as large as a gaff hook that they use in saltwater fishing to get the fish in the boat.

My brother David didn't like running his hand under those rocks or up in the hollow logs because snakes just didn't agree with him. So, I always had him stand with his feet blocking the exit hole. David always had his trusty slingshot with him so I never had to worry about snakes coming up behind me. I'm not just bragging but David was the best slingshot artist I have ever seen. He was a natural left hander who was deadly whether his target was standing still or moving. One time, on the way to the river, we were bouncing over field rows when a big "cane cutter" rabbit came running out. Using split shot lead for ammo; David got the rabbit with one shot.

But, back to my story, we hadn't gone fifty yards up the river before we came to the big flat rock, called "Two Story". I ran my bumpin' hook in the bottom hole while David stood guard. All at once a fine six pound blue catfish got all tangled up in David's bell bottomed britches legs. We took our supper back to the truck, built a fire, skinned the rabbit and the fish, and had a wonderful meal. I told David that folks would not believe how successful you could be with just a slingshot and a pair of bell-bottomed britches.

On May 8, 1977, Dad asked me if I might be interested in a twelve foot aluminum boat that he had seen for sale. Dad knew me like a book. He had already bought that boat, six bicycles, and three antique outboard motors. I paid him fifty dollars for the boat, and he sold the bicycles for a profit. That boat had seen some rough use over the years, but to me it was beautiful. It didn't take long to discover that one of my most important pieces of equipment on this "ship" would be a small one or two gallon bucket for bailing out water. Naming my boat was easy, but my "Titanic" has seen far more navigation time, over the years, than its namesake. Every time someone new goes fishing with me, the first thing that happens is, they see their feet slowly being submerged. They then ask if my boat leaks and I answer, "Like a cow pissing on a flat rock". There is really nothing wrong with this boat, it just thinks it's a submarine. The sinking problem might be something to worry about on any other river, but the Sipsey is different. If you sink in the "Titanic", in order to keep from drowning, all you have to do is stand up.

Dad loved to fish, but he didn't like getting wet, which is part of going fishing in the "Titanic". He would much rather go to the Tennessee River, Smith Lake, or the Gulf Coast. He always kept a good bass boat or a pleasure craft that you could ski behind. On one trip to the mouth of Little River to set out hooks, he did brave the perils of fishing in the "Titanic". May 3, 1980, found us running our hooks on a beautiful sun splashed morning. We caught six fish, three blue catfish, two spotted catfish {or flatheads for those who don't know about spotted cats} and one big soft shelled turtle. That turtle was so big he wouldn't even come close to fitting in a five gallon bucket. As soon as Dad put him in the boat, he flipped him over on his back, and that old turtle became as calm as could be. Dad told me to go get the truck and bring it down river to a place called "three beeches", and he would float the boat on down the river.

It took me a while to walk to the truck and then drive around the gravel road, but I thought he would be there waiting for me. When I got there, there was no sign of him.

I waited for a while, but then I got worried and started hiking back up the river. I knew something must be wrong and just as I rounded a bend in the river, there was Dad standing on a very limber tree that had fallen across the river. I asked him what had happened and Dad said while he was trying to get the boat over the tree, the turtle had turned over, got on his feet, and wouldn't let him back in the boat. To solve this problem, Dad told me to cut a pole so he could flip the turtle back over on his back. On the way home I asked Dad why he didn't just get back in the boat, and to explain his reasoning he told me this story.

His story went like this, "Kenneth Guin owned the drug store in Carbon Hill and he had hired a young man to sweep the floors, stock shelves, and do other odd jobs around the pharmacy. One day Mr. Guin had to run to the bank and he told his hired help to tell any customers who came in that he would be right back. Soon a man in a suit and tie came rushing in and asked to buy some cough medicine. The young man told him the pharmacist would be back soon, but the poor man was coughing so bad that he felt sorry for him and sold him some medicine and he went away. When Mr. Guin returned he asked if he had missed any customers and the young man told him about the customer who needed cough medicine. Mr. Guin asked what he had sold him and the helper went behind the counter and picked up a bottle of laxative. Mr. Guin exclaimed, "Boy, that isn't cough medicine!" The young man said, "Yes, but look at that man on the corner, leaning against the light post. He's afraid to cough now!"

*"Noodling" Jackie H., Dustin H., Dillon H., Derek T., Heath T.,
Chad H., Roy Dale T., and Derm T.*

Chapter Seven

Corks, Bobbers and Floats

I have always loved watching a cork do a dance on the water. They actually try to tell you what's going on down below. A bass will slowly pull the cork down and away. Catfish are more aggressive and leave faster. Bream want to dance. They will make that cork do more moves than you can believe. Crappies are fashion designers. They like very colorful corks. Trout can be tough to catch, if the float is too big. Whether it is a cork, bobber, or float really doesn't matter. What is important is that you understand the meaning behind the dance. I learned early in life that if you take your eyes off the float, most likely your bait will be gone.

I have spent many hours watching and waiting for the action part of a movie to come and I have had some pretty good ideas come to mind while watching, but you can't write and watch at the same time, so most are forgotten. One night I was watching the National Geographic channel and they were showing some folks over in Southeast Asia fishing for the Mekong giant catfish. They strung a long net out in the river and had some football size floats on top of the net. The floats would start bouncing when they had a fish. These folks were patient, but they were also thrifty. After they put out their nets, they made baskets as they waited. Now, if there's the slightest chance that I might catch a giant catfish, those floats would have my undivided attention. I guess some folks are just in too big of a hurry, but at least it got them on T.V.

I have always been good at watching and waiting. For eleven years I owned a small service station in my home town of Eldridge, Al. I have watched thousands of cars and trucks go past on Highway 78 and waited for them to stop in for a little old-fashioned service. You know the kind where your oil is checked, your gas is pumped, your tires are aired up, and your windshield is washed. It seems to me that the high price of gas would be easier to take if someone would wash your windshield once in a while.

My dad owned this service station from 1960-1977. In the early years the little station didn't have indoor plumbing and the only facility it had was a little outhouse out back. One day Dad was sitting on the whittling bench in front of the station when a big, shiny car came sliding in with gravel flying and dust boiling. The car door flew open and a long, lanky fellow jumped out. He was all dressed up in his suit and tie and was wearing a fine, grey felt hat. In a great hurry, he asked where the bathrooms were located. Dad told him they were around at the back and tried to tell him to wait a minute, but he was already around the corner. In a little the dust settled, the birds started back singing, and Dad went back to his whittling. The man came around the corner with his grey felt hat in his hand and a very red welt across his forehead. Dad told him, "Doggone mister, I'm sorry. I tried to stop you to tell you about my wife's clothesline that's stretched out back there". The man said, "Oh, that's all right. I wouldn't have made it anyway".

That station was a great place to plan a fishing trip. Kinfolks, high school buddies, friends, and their sons all came to listen to the stories, share the laughs, and enjoy a place that America forgot. Some of my earliest memories are of the little two pump station with a grease rack on the east side for changing oil and repairing flat tires. Dad always had a red grease rag in his back pocket and I just naturally had to have one too.

Not too long ago one of "my boys" asked me what my most important piece of equipment was. I told him that it was, without a doubt, my red grease rag. He wanted to know if the rag was more important than my Ole Blue, my Chevy 4 W.D. I said, "Yes". He was still skeptical and asked if it was more important than the "Titanic". I replied, "Yes". I then explained the reason for my answers. "When we go fishing we always have to wipe the worm dirt, or chicken liver off our hands. When we catch a big catfish or gar, they are a whole lot easier to hold onto with that red rag. However, the most important reason is, If you have to wipe your bottom with dry leaves or a red rag, the red rag will win every time".

Every outdoors man knows those pesky "skeeters" can give you all kinds of trouble. On May 30, 1972, I was at the Blue Hole on Mallard Creek. It is one of the most beautiful places I know to sit, on the bank, with a cane pole, cork, hook, and line. The moss is six inches deep, and the sun rarely reaches beneath the canopy of giant Beech and Hemlock trees. The creek runs deep down a canyon of mists and shadows.

On this particular day, the fishing was slow, so I had time to sit back and do some serious thinking. I had my trusty red rag in action, keeping the "skeeters" at bay. I got to thinking that if a fellow had a light weight shoulder harness with an extension that would go up behind your head, and this had a slit at the end of it, to put a red grease rag in, you could turn it on, and it would whirl around, totally discouraging any bug from ruining your outing. Of course, the little motor would be run by batteries. That way your arm wouldn't feel like a baseball pitcher who had just thrown 119 innings.

I could even write the advertising for it. It would be totally natural, no chemicals, no smelly fumes, and it could even stir up a breeze to keep you cool in hot weather. You could get one dozen red rags and free safety glasses with it, if you call right now. The whole rig would cost only $19.95, and you would receive the U. R. A Sucker guarantee. My little bug deterrent would be called the "Whirl Away Skeeter Deterrent".

It is always a thrill to have "my boys" come back for a visit. The older ones now have wives and children to keep their lives in a whirlwind, but they always find time to slip off to the river for another adventure. They come home fully prepared. Suits and ties are discarded and liberty overalls, with red rags in the back pockets, are put on. I take this wardrobe change as a compliment. It sure makes me proud to see them all grown up, but they still remember where they came from.

Casey Farris comes all the way from Houston, Texas, to enjoy being surrounded by family and friends. His wife, Tammy, has a special memory of my mom's little log cabin, located on my "sprinkle hole" place, not far from the lazy water of the Sipsey River. That is where Casey proposed to her, and now two beautiful children have joined the Farris family.

About four years ago, Casey and crew came back to Alabama for a visit. A fishing trip and a family get together were quickly planned, with a meal at the cabin. Casey and Tammy were riding home with in ol' Blue, and I asked Casey if Tammy had ever been through the Red Tucker Ford. He answered no but he thought it would do her good. Now the Red Tucker Ford is simply a place to cross the creek where there is no bridge. As you ride down the gravel road to the ford, you notice that the creek bottom is solid rock and about as smooth as going down concrete stairs in a log truck. My truck has big knobby tires and that makes the ride even rougher. Tammy sat in the middle, and she bounced all over the inside of that truck. Have you ever seen a Christian lady try to keep from bouncing? It sure makes them red in the face. We tried not to burst out laughing, but it was really hard. About nine months later their son Will was born. I guess if I advertised the power of an ol' blue truck, a pretty girl, and the Red Tucker Ford, "Viagra" would go out of business.

Chapter Eight

....

Lines of Time

The strength of your line and the quality of the knot has to work together as one to be successful in fishing. I frequently check my line for abrasions that would weaken the strength of it. I can say, in all honesty, that over the years few fish have broken my line. It has happened, and believe me, nothing is more humbling. The knot that connects the line to the hook is just as important as how strong the line is and there are more ways to tie a knot than you can count.

"Tying the knot" is an expression everyone connects with getting married. The ten children of Law Donald and Linnie Mae Hendrix, my grandparents, have all celebrated at least fifty years of marriage. Mom and Dad had sixty two years together, and they were a great pair. Although some of the ten Hendrix children are gone now, their children, grandchildren, and a host of other relatives still gather each year to enjoy good fellowship, and the telling of old family stories.

Papa Hendrix was a hard-working sawmill man. One day he was driving down the road and he saw a very large lady walking to town. He stopped to give her a lift and she climbed in and started telling him her troubles. She was upset because folks talked about her husband being ugly. She said, "He can't help his looks, a mule kicked him in the face". When Papa came home and told the family about it he said, "It's too bad Mr. Bice didn't shoot that mule before it kicked the whole family in the face." As we all know, a well placed "line" can speak volumes in any conversation.

My mom's first name is Iva. Sometimes, she gives a unique twist to the conversation, and I call these sayings "Iva'isms". Recently, we were going through a large box of pictures and one caught her eye. It was a photo of the torch bearer carrying the Olympic flame through our town on its way to Los Angeles. She said, "Oh, there's the flame thrower." One day when I came home from work Mom told me a Clint Eastwood movie was coming on T.V. that night. [She knows I love his movies.] I asked her which one and she replied, "A Pocketful of Money" but I knew she meant, "A Fistful of Dollars". Mom is a consummate optimist. One of her favorite sayings also came from a Clint Eastwood movie. The phrase is "Endeavor to Persevere", but Mom always says, "Persevere to endure". When the National Geographic channel shows those giant black beetles pushing a ball of dung around Mom says, "There's old hockey pot". I came from fishing one evening and "Jeopardy" was on. Mom asked me what was contained in a humble scam. I knew the answer, even though the question was wrong. She meant to say, "What is contained in a camel's hump?"

I love getting little notes in my lunch box, occasionally, from Mom. I carefully read each one and add it to my collection. One day, I opened the box and found a note that simply said, "~~High,~~" "~~Hay,~~" "~~Hey,~~" "Hi." These simple things bring a smile to my face every time.

"Going to the beach," is a well known expression that brings to mind sand, sea, sun, and pretty girls in skimpy swimsuits, but an old fishing buddy of mine had his own unique twist to this phrase. Rusty Whitehead was as country as cornbread and buttermilk. He was a great fisherman with a wonderful sense of humor, and he spoke with a very slow southern drawl that gave each word a touch of silver. Rusty loved to tell about his first marriage. He told his new bride to have everything packed and ready to go, because as soon as the "I do's" had been said they were going to the beach. Finally the newlyweds were on their way. But, instead of going to the coast, Rusty's old pickup headed straight to the trestle bottoms by the Sipsey River, where the biggest "beech" tree in all of Fayette County stood. Rusty would grin and say that they stayed a whole week and lived happily ever after.

Mom has a faded old postcard with the phrase "Familiar Scenes in Dixie" printed on it. There are five different pictures depicted on the card. My dad is in the middle picture. It shows him ankle deep in the gulf, casting his line into the surf. We had taken a vacation to Gulf Shores State Park and while Dad was fishing, someone had taken his picture. Several months later we stopped at a cafe in Carbon Hill, Alabama. I was looking through some postcards in a rack and my heart skipped a beat when I spotted Dad's picture on the card. The rod and reel he used on that trip are proudly displayed in my angler's chest.

That picture has Dad frozen in full stride, casting his line. His line transcends the years and brings so many wonderful memories to mind. The postcard probably cost no more than a dime back then, but to me it is priceless and perfectly frames the lines of time.

Chapter Nine

The Reel Drawer

I'm always a little sad when I pull open the reel drawer. Each reel in there is an old friend, fishing buddies that are not able to perform like they once did. I have always loved Zebco reels. (My dad preferred Johnson or Pfulger reels.) I don't have any expensive reels. Most of mine are "blue collar workers". I know some fishermen who would never bank fish or wade the creek with their rod and reel. They might get it dirty or, heaven forbid, get it wet.

I have always kept my reels in top notch condition, but the problem is I just flat wear them out. Zebco could have made me a field tester, because if they hold up to the constant use I put them through, then they should last a long, long time. The best reels I have used were 802 Zebcos, and I used them on every bank fishing trip I made. Bank fishing is not a gentle way to fish. Most times you bait your hook, cast it out, and then jab the butt of the rod down into the muddy bank.

Along about the first of April, every year, a very good friend, J.T,

Tidwell, reminds me that he has a birthday coming up. J.T. really loves to fish, and even though he has six grown children, I am the one who gets him fishing gear. One year Zebco came out with a new rod with a fancy pistol grip that was supposed to make it easier to hold, so I bought him the complete outfit, reel and rod, for his birthday. He surely was pleased, and a fishing trip for that afternoon was planned. We went down to J.T.'s favorite place to bank fish, the Skiff Landing hole on the Sipsey River. As soon as we baited our hooks we cast toward the far bank, and J.T. took his brand new rod and reel and tried to jab it into the bank, without success. He tried again and again, each time with a little more force. Finally he said, "Dadgum, Don Tucker, this rod and reel don't stick in the bank like it should." After I stopped laughing, I cut him a forked stick to hold his rod, so he could watch it tip when he got a bite.

Some years ago, J.T. was fitted with some brand, new dentures. Now as everyone who has had dentures knows, it takes a while to break them in, just like a new pair of shoes. We were fishing down on the river, and J.T. would pull those dentures out and start whittling on them. I would advise him to stop whittling on them and just get used to them, but he would remind me that it was his jaw hurting, not mine. About a week later, on a bright Saturday morning, J.T. woke up in agony, and he was ready to go to a dentist, any dentist, anywhere. He had all his kids calling everywhere, trying to find a dentist who was open on Saturday. Finally, a dentist was located, way up in north Alabama. This particular dentist usually just saw little children as patients, but since this was an emergency, he said he would see J.T. His son, Roy Dale, drove him up there and when they got to the office the waiting room was full of little kids and their mamas, but they took J.T. right on back. Roy Dale said that every time his dad hollered the kid's eyes just about rolled back in their heads. After a while, a little boy came out from seeing the dentist, and he had great, big tears rolling down his cheeks. His mom hugged him and asked if they had hurt him that bad. He said, "No, they didn't hurt me, but they are killing that old man in the next room!"

My mom told me about one of the most unusual errands she had ever gone on. She and Dad had not been married long, and they had just sat down to supper at Dad's parents house when Granddad Tucker said, "Doggone, I have left my teeth in the creek". Evidently, his new dentures had been bothering him and he had placed his new "store bought" teeth on a flat rock there in the cool water. Mom and Dad volunteered to go teeth hunting and they were exactly where Granddad said they were. Mom said those teeth surely did look funny lying there on that flat rock, just shining in the moonlight.

Over the years, I have been honored to wet a line with some really great fishermen. I remember when I was six or seven years old I kept a cane pole baited in the small branch that ran beside the service station. Dad's uncle Murray had caught a big bass and he put him on my hook. Now, that little branch could not have been more than six inches deep, but I was convinced that it held a world record catch just waiting for me to snag him. It pays to be patient and confident. I have told folks that I believed I could catch fish out of a mud puddle.

Each year when our family has our reunion, I am officially in charge of the fishing for the kids. I know Bill Dance and Roland Martin have fished in some pressure packed tournaments, but you haven't experienced pressure until you find yourself trying to help a dozen five to eight year olds catch a fish. Now, I'm not talking about big fish. The kids don't care how big it is as long as it is a fish. I try my best to give them the confidence they need to keep trying, but sometimes all the confidence, patience, and optimism in the world are as useless as an empty tackle box.

May 19, 1996, found me on the river bank at the Sprinkle deep hole for some night bank fishing with my cousins, Kyle and Casey. We baited our hooks and cast out our lines. I caught a nice five pound blue catfish, and Kyle caught his twin brother. Poor ol' Casey, however, couldn't get a bite. I told him to be patient and stay confident. Meanwhile, Kyle and I got a few more bites but no fish. Casey was patient, but after an hour without a bite, his patience was gone. I suggested he might want to check his hook to see if he still had bait. He began to reel in his line and discovered that instead of his hook being in the water; it had been hung up in a tree branch, ten feet above him.

Casey has a snack while he and Don show off the night's catch.

Chapter Ten

....

Set Hooks and Throw Lines

I keep my set hooks and throw lines in the bottom center of the angler's chest, behind the double doors. The set hooks or limb-lines are wound on a 14 inch board. My old boat, the "Titanic", had seen so much use, over the years that I had to replace the worn out wooden seats with new treated lumber. Being the sentimental type, I cut the worn out seats into boards and wound my set hooks on them. The set hooks are 130 pound test, three to six feet long of braided line with a lead weight and 4-0 to 6-0 mustad hooks tied on them. The throw lines consist of a brick tied to one of a thirty foot length of 300 pound test nylon line. Seven to ten 4-0 to 6-0 hooks hang from foot long lengths of braided line, tied to the main line. To deploy it, you simply find a snag or a root close to the bank, tie it off, and then unwind the main line from the brick. You bait your hooks as you go. Once the line is tight, you drop the brick at the end of the line. I try to have all my hooks set out before dark. Then I find a big flat rock or gravel bar, and eat my hotdogs and cake. I try to wait at least an hour before I run my hooks, to either rebait or take fish off. This is just like Christmas to me, because you never know what you will find on the hooks. This is my favorite kind of fishing.

The Sipsey River is a small stream compared to other Alabama rivers, but the variety and abundance of fish make it a special treasure. I have seen this river produce some amazingly large fish. On May 15, 2004, Eric Aultman, Wesley Tucker, and I caught a 42 lb.-8oz flathead catfish on one of my throw lines.

On the same date, 26 years earlier, my friend, Tucson Stovall and I set out hooks at the mouth of Mallard Creek. We already had three fine flathead catfish flopping in the boat and Tucson was checking the lines while I paddled us down river. Ol' Tucson said, "We got us another one, "Tucky Lucky", as I eased him up to a bouncing cane pole. I told him to pull it in quick, because even though the water was deep, there were several big logs on the bottom so he grabbed that line and swung it in the boat. What hit the bottom of the boat was not a catfish but a four foot long eel. Tucson abandoned ship! I looked toward the bank and there stood Tucson. He had crossed twenty feet of water that was at least ten feet deep, and yet, he was only wet up to his ankles. A few years later Ol' Tucson became a preacher and the devil lost a good right arm. I like to think that eel helped Tucson find religion.

I like to set my set hooks and throw lines out in deep water or close to it. The big fish like to hang out where food and cover are present. September 9, 2004, my crew of Adam, Eric, and Alex Aultman and myself went to Gorman's for some set hook fishing fun. These boys make a great crew. Their feet are so big; they cover up most of the holes in the bottom of the old "Titanic". They are so tall (Adam is 6'7", Eric is 6'4", and Alex is 6'5) that all they have to do to keep from drowning is stand up. I tell them the river mud makes them grow tall.

On this particular trip they brought a friend, B.J., with them from school. Anytime you have five or more people in a twelve foot, flat bottom boat, you will find that sinking is a constant threat. It was B.J.'s first time to set hooks, so the job of bailing water fell on him. Now, you might think that would not be a hard job, but it sure is frustrating. By the time you scoop out a gallon of water and toss it overboard, the water level is up again. That boy did not like his job, but that night and the next morning, when we were catching fish, he didn't complain. When we made pictures of our fish, everyone was grinning all over their faces. Those three Aultman boys make as fine a crew as this old river rat could ask for, and they are proud to be called my boys.

The threesome of Dustin Haley, Chase O'Mary, and Heath Tidwell, make up another favorite crew. These three cousins are sons of friends of mine, and I have watched them grow up. July 8, 2000, was the first time they set out hooks with me, and I knew right away that they would be special. We put our hooks out and talked about the big ones we were going to catch. As kinfolks, especially cousins are apt to do; those three were constantly fussing at each other. When we started to check our hooks, we didn't have to go far before we saw one of our cane poles pulling down. All three were giving orders on what to do, and they managed to let a really big gar get away. The lessons they should have learned quickly were too soon forgotten, and when we got to "round rock shoal", we didn't have a single fish to photograph. On the way home, I told them to cheer up, because the next morning we would have a big one. Sure enough, when we rounded the bend in the river, and cruised into the hollow log hole the next day, the cane pole, stuck firmly in the bank, was dancing steadily up and down. I stopped the boat and told them to work together this time, and smooth as silk, all three working as one, they put the fifteen to twenty pound, flathead catfish in the boat. I gave each of them a big "Don Tucker" pat on the back, and told them that if they worked together, there wasn't anything they couldn't accomplish. Now they look at each other and see a special friend.

I learned to set out hooks from the old masters, J.T. Tidwell and Rusty Whitehead, who had grown up together. They had been good friends for years, but their friendship had become strained over a piece of land. I would have loved to be able to set hooks out with both of them in the boat with me because they knew the Sipsey River and understood its' timeless rhythm. Reading the current, knowing the eddy holes, finding rock and log structures, and where to set out hooks, was second nature to them. J.T. would listen to a suggestion, but not Rusty. It was Rusty's way, or no way. I was always trying to persuade him to not set his hooks so deep. Rusty would just grin and say, "Son, you have to put the bait down deep, because that's where the fish are." I would reply that catfish have eyes on top of their heads. Ol' Rusty would laugh and hang 'em deep, and many times I had to dive to the bottom to untangle a fish for him.

Rusty didn't tie his hooks to cane poles; he said they were too flimsy and a big fish would pull them out of the bank. As soon as we got to where we were going to fish, Rusty would take out his pocket knife, and cut poles to tie his lines on. These poles were young trees, thick around as a fifty cent piece, and twelve to sixteen feet long. He was one of the strongest men I have ever known, and when he stuck that pole in the bank, you could not pull it out. I have seen these saplings sprout, and I tell the boys that the trees leaning over the river used to be fishing poles.

August 8, 1980, we set hooks at the "sprinkle deep hole". The next morning, as we were running our hooks, Rusty said that a big fish had pulled one of his poles out of the bank. I told him there wasn't a fish in the river big enough to pull out one of his poles. He asked me to paddle the boat around to see if we could find it, and after two or three trips around the deep hole, I found his pole. I was laughing so hard as I showed him the two inches of pole sticking out of the bank. An old beaver had gnawed his pole off and that left Rusty as mad as a hornet.

Chapter Eleven

Memories on Film

Displayed on the top and on the wall behind the "Angler's chest" are several pictures, each sporting its own fishing frame. Every picture has a story to tell. "Fishing in the mist" is a picture of me standing knee deep in the frigid water below the Smith Lake dam. Another is of me holding a fine three pound rainbow trout, caught on the very same trip, June 7, 2002. There are also several pictures of me holding big flathead catfish caught on the Sipsey River. One picture, I'm proud to display, is of two of my "superstar" giggers, Adam Aultman and Chad Henderson, holding a huge gar that is almost as long as they are tall. On a wade fishing trip to Box's creek, August 3, 2003, I caught a fine, four pound, spotted bass. Each time I look at that picture I can relive that fight again.

The first time a camera was taken to the river, was on a float fishing trip with Bartley Wyers, in August of 1988. Bartley had brought along a camera that was considerably more valuable than the "one time use" cameras that I buy. The fishing that day was just so-so, but that camera brought the fishing to life like nothing else could. I'm no ace photographer, by any means, but I know that if you want to see a boy grin all the way around his head, make his picture holding a fish that he just caught or gigged.

I have held an annual camp out at my Sprinkle hole property since 1999. About twenty men and boys from church, and their friends gather to see who can get wetter and muddier down on the Sipsey River. Every year I buy fifteen pounds of frog legs to fry up golden brown and, to them, we add all kinds of good food. After all are fed, the whole group heads for the river bank. I always have a rock skipping contest and a river run. Prizes for the winners are gold dollars and pocket knives. We also have a barrel bull suspended above the river for those who really like a challenge. Only two have ridden it for the full eight seconds, Bobby Hallmark and Alex Aultman. When they received their prize money of eight gold dollars, the picture perfectly captured their joy of winning. Dillon Haley will someday have quite a collection of pocket knives for winning the rock skipping contest. I always make several pictures and give them to the boys, so thy can hold on to their youth as long as possible.

Don with "camp out" medal winners , Clay and Austin.

Not long ago I was watching funny videos on T.V. and one video showed a group of kindergarten kids all dressed to graduate. Each one was asked what they want to be when they grow up. They had all kinds of answers, but one little boy had the perfect answer. He said, "I don't want to grow up!"

A co-worker was standing in line waiting to clock out the other day, and he was fussing about having to take his car to the insurance adjuster so it could be photographed, so I told him about a friend of mine who had the same problem. My friend's sixteen year old daughter had just gotten her learner's permit when she announced her desire for a new car. He tried in vain to dissuade her, but she had her heart set on it and before long she had her new car. A week after she got the new car, she was happily driving her car, talking on her cell phone, and changing stations on the radio, and then my friend received the call from her that the new car was in a ditch. All the way to the accident scene, my friend was very angry, because he had felt that this would happen. He was glad that his wife was away because she would have panicked when they got the call. When he arrived at the scene and saw that the car was totaled, the anger he felt over an accident he was powerless to avoid was etched on his face As he looked at his little girl, he asked, "Well Heather, what do you want me to do about this?" With tears streaming down her face, Heather sobbed, "Tell MaMa you did it."

A photograph can become a special treasure to the angler who catches the biggest fish. I am not a professional photographer, but I do try to get the right amount of light and not cut someone's head off, or take a picture of their feet. I pose them with their fish and I believe any picture is better than none. I tell the boys that someday they will have something to show their grandchildren. When they ask me about the big fish I have caught over the years, I always tell them that I have caught some of the biggest fish ever to come out of the Sipsey River. Then I tell them about one fish that was so big, the picture weighed seven pounds!

The power of a photograph can change a person's life and make it worth living. My uncle, Clyde Welch, was a perfect example of this. Clyde married my mom's sister, Octavia Marie, and they were a splendid pair. Clyde was tall with broad shoulders and handsome and Tava would make any man's heart skip a beat. While Clyde was stationed in the South Pacific, during World War II, Tava sent him her version of the famous, Betty Grable pose. It's a wonder Clyde didn't wipe out the entire Japanese military, single handed, just so he could come home. That picture is a cherished family memento and it will bring a smile to many generations that spring from their love.

With the help of the "one time use" cameras I have taken thousands of pictures, most of them of wet, muddy boys holding fish. I try to keep one handy, because you never know when a "once in a lifetime" shot might present itself. The best photo I have ever taken was when my dad and I were down on the Sprinkle hole property doing a little dove hunting. It was September 27, 1997, and Dad had driven his 3600 Ford Tractor down there to do some bush hogging in the bottom field. I positioned my Chevy 4WD under the big oak tree at the end of the hill field and put the tail gate down so we would have a place to sit. There was a nice breeze blowing, and Dad felt like getting his picture taken. I made several of him shouldering his shotgun, and he seemed really happy to be there. We hadn't been there long before three doves came flying straight down the field toward us. Dad coolly shouldered his gun and nailed all three. I didn't even think about my gun or anything else, but getting great pictures of my Dad.

As the afternoon faded toward evening, I drove to the upper end of the bottom field as Dad came riding up on his tractor. (You can see the whole bottom field from that spot.) Dad threw his hand up to wave "good-bye" as he left the freshly mowed field. With a big smile on his face, he headed home to supper. Less than a month later, he fell and broke his hip, and while in surgery to repair it, he suffered a stroke. That photo is the last one of my dad while he still had a measure of good health. The next three years of his life were one long nightmare of pain and confusion. Mom had that picture enlarged and placed it on the night table by her bed, with love. I see a very simple message from my Dad when I look at that picture, "My work here is done, and I'm moving on".

Chapter Twelve

Flies and Ties

The lower right hand drawer of the angler's chest contains my fly fishing tackle. The first time I held a fly rod in my hand, was on a trip to the Blue Ridge Mountains in east Tennessee and North Carolina. I was six or seven years old and this was my first trip out of the state. All the way to the mountains I kept asking if we would see a bear. Dad kept assuring me that we would. As the miles dragged on, I was sure we would never get there.

Finally, as we were inching along on the most crooked road I had ever seen, we rounded a curve and a big ol' bear came bouncing across the road. Dad grabbed his old Kodak movie camera and started shooting and in his excitement he was moving the camera much too fast. He chased that bear, on film, all the way down that mountain. When we watched the movie on Dad's old Bell & Howell projector, all you could see of that bear was his big, black, bottom bouncing through the woods.

When we entered North Carolina, a sign on the side of the road advertised a trout pond with the amounts of $1.50 per pound and $1.50 to fish. Dad turned up the long driveway and stopped at a beautiful little log cabin next to a sparkling, clear, four to five acre pond. The trout were as thick as hair on a dog's back, and it looked like you could just reach out and scoop one up with your hands. The old gentleman sitting on the porch told Dad that kernel corn from a can would do for bait. Dad handed me an old rod and reel that would have been classified as yard sale junk. Mom and Dad leisurely fished around the pond, but I couldn't even get my hook in the water. The old gentleman saw that I was having problems, so he came walking up with a split bamboo rod and Phulgar reel. It was the most beautiful thing I had ever seen. He told me to use it just like a cane pole, swing it out, and pull the fish in, no casting. I knew how to use a cane pole and it showed. Mom told Dad that he might want to quit, because Don already had a mess of fish. Dad tried to talk the man into letting him put some of the fish back, but he said they would just die. As we drove down the road, Mom suggested that we stop at the overlook and have a fish supper. Dad and I cleaned the fish and Mom worked her magic cooking them. As we ate our supper, looking out over the beautiful Blue Ridge Mountains, Dad commented that this was the best $38.50 he had ever spent.

Family ties run deep on both sides of our family. The Tucker reunion is held on the third Saturday in May at the old Hopewell Cemetery. My great, great grand father George Tucker, who fought in the Revolutionary War as a lieutenant and was a member of Morgan's riflemen, is buried there. He was born in 1745, in Amelia County, Virginia, and died in 1852, in Marion County, Alabama. He and his wife raised ten children, and every one of them had a large family. My

Dad said, "Everybody used to be Tuckers before they started lying and stealing".

The love of fishing began on family trips to the Tennessee River. Here the author is with his cousin, Carol Tucker.

The Tucker reunion is much different from the Hendrix reunion. The Hendrix clan are all close kin, while the Tuckers have to have a book to "cipher" out the connections. Many of the Tuckers are genealogists who just love to explore the many branches of our family tree. (A few years ago, my niece Kara was to be married to Curtis Kwasniewski and my cousin was to read the announcement at Church on Sunday morning. Marcus, like many of us, has a hard time pronouncing some names, but he gave it his best shot. He said he was happy to announce the up-coming marriage of Kara to Curtis Kawasaki. I told Mom that I did not know Kara was marrying a Japanese-Polish guy.) There is one thing about having a large family, you will always have friends to help you through the valleys and cheer you over the hills.

Two weeks before Christmas in 1996, I was talking to some of my co-workers at work when our boss, Kevin Seals, came walking in and asked what we would like to have for Christmas. I told him that I would like to build a little log cabin for my Mom, on my "Sprinkle Hole" place, if I had the money. He said if I really wanted to do that I should pick a spot for it and get some friends together to help. Not long after I bought the land in 1989 Mom had told Dad that she would like to put a little cabin in a certain spot, so I made some phone calls and several of my friends and family wanted to help.

Dad was in the hospital with pneumonia and Mom was taking care of him so she didn't know what we were doing. It took us four days to build a sixteen by twenty cabin with a fine front porch. (How can you repay folks for helping to make Christmas special for your mom?) Christmas morning I drove her to the place and as we entered the gate I asked her to close her eyes. It must have seemed to take forever for us to drive around the fields to reach the cabin. I will never forget the joy on her face when I told her to open her eyes. It is one of my happiest memories and we have had many good times there. A wheelchair ramp was added later so Dad and others would be able to enjoy it.

Before long, Mom told me I needed to build an outhouse because there was no water or electricity at the cabin. I figured I had used up all my favors, so I decided to build it myself. It went up better than I expected it would, and when I had it almost finished I asked Mom to ride with me to see the outhouse. I still needed to cut the quarter moon in the door and the hole in the seat. I asked her how big I should cut the hole for the seat, because I had forgotten to measure the toilet seat at home. She asked for my pencil, sat down on the seat and drew a circle around those Hendrix hips. I started laughing and told her if I made the hole that big I would fall in. Hendrix women are known for their good cooking.

I would never intentionally embarrass my mom, and I try not to embarrass myself, but I feel so comfortable in my Liberty overalls and Mom would rather I wear a shirt and pants. A float fishing trip, April 13, 2002, will prove this point. My friend J.T. Tidwell, (who is almost more comfortable in overalls than I am), his grandson Heath, and I had just ended a great day of fishing on the river, and we stopped at a little service station for a cold drink. There were several friends there that we had known for years. They knew that we had been fishing and wanted to see our full stringer of fish. Before long J.T. and I were telling jokes and fishing stories and everyone was really laughing at us and enjoying our company. As we were driving home I said that if I had an audience that appreciated my jokes that much I would be rich in no time. J.T. said, "Don Tucker, we should go on tour together." Heath said, "You two, don't get your hopes up. They were laughing because both your flies were open!"

Chapter Thirteen

....

Hot Spots

All successful fishermen have their own special places to fish that are almost guaranteed to produce a full stringer. My problem is that I spend too much time enjoying those special spots. If I didn't have to work for a living I would practically live there. Mom understands how much fishing means to me but, she doesn't like me fishing on Sunday. I try to be there on Sunday morning, but come Sunday night the old Sipsey River is calling me.

One Sunday night I was late getting to church services, again. That night after supper, Mom told me a joke that I should take to heart. It was about a big city lawyer who died and went to heaven. He was standing at the pearly gate waiting to pass through and when it was his turn, Saint Peter asked him what good he had done in his life. The old lawyer said that while he was in college he had seen a homeless person and he gave him a quarter. Saint Peter told Gabriel to go down to earth and check out his story. Gabriel returned and said that the old lawyer was telling the truth. Saint Peter then asked if he had done any other good deeds. The old lawyer said yes, once, when he was walking out of the Social Security office he saw a hungry man and gave him a quarter. Again, Saint Peter sent Gabriel down to check out his story, and Gabriel returned to say this was also the truth. Then, Saint Peter turned to Gabriel and asked what he thought should be done with the man. Gabriel replied, "Give him back his fifty cents, and tell him to go to hell."

Sometimes, being late to church is totally out of my control. My old Chevy is thirty years old and it is showing its age. A while back it needed a new drive shaft. When my friend, Scot Tucker came to pick it up in his new car hauler, he asked me to go for a ride and check it out. The temperature outside was ninety-eight degrees. I was impressed with the air conditioner and I was cool all over, with the exception of my bottom. I finally told Scot that he must have a bad muffler because it was hot enough to fry an egg on my seat. He started laughing and told me to look for the seat warmer button on the side of the seat and turn it off. I had accidentally turned it on when I got into the truck.

Summer time in Alabama can be brutal. When it's hot, I always find time to go float fishing on the Sipsey River. The Sipsey is most beautiful in late spring and fall. In summer, when the water level is lowest, a fun time can turn into work, pulling the "Titanic" over logs and shoals. I have learned as I've grown older that the aches and pains I feel are almost equal to the number of fish I catch.

I do so love to fish and it is even more fun when the young folks are present. June 17, 2005, I loaded up ol' Blue with my niece, Jenny, and her two girls, Mallory and Baylie, to go to Gorman's for a float fishing trip. I discovered that the girls love to get wet and muddy, just like the boys, and it is probably going to happen in the "Titanic." Mallory caught several bream and then a big one broke her line. I think Baylie could make a good "ship's captain" someday by the way she handles a paddle. When it was time to go home, I had Jenny drive ol' Blue and pull the boat up the bank. Mallory and Baylie were amazed to see that their mom could handle that truck so easily. It was a fun trip and I think times like this can help bond families together, even though they may not happen very often.

Thanksgiving has always been a time of coming together for my family. One Thanksgiving, a small convoy of cars followed ol' Blue to my "red gate" place, next to the river. We left the cars and vans parked at the gate, and everyone climbed in my truck. The kids had never ridden in the back of a pickup truck before, so it was quite an adventure for them. Kara's son, Jacob, was in the back, behind me and could see me in the side mirror. As we were bouncing along the dirt road, he said, "Don, it sure is windy back here!" One thing I like about kids is that you don't have to wonder what is on their mind.

One July, a wind storm had blown down two huge trees in one of my fields in "Walker Bottoms". On a blistering hot Saturday I was cutting up the trees with a power saw, when I started seeing those little black spots that tell you it's time to cool off. I headed for the mouth of Little River where it meets with New River to become the Sipsey. Now, skinny dipping might not be something you would want to do in a crowded pool, but it should be all right when you are four miles in the middle of nowhere. I'm sitting on a submerged log close to the bank with only my head above the water when I hear someone talking. Looking up river I spot six canoes floating down toward me. The first five canoes go slowly by. Then as the sixth one is passing, a young boy about eight spots me and says, "Mister, this water sure is clear, isn't it?"

Wade fishing is a sure way to beat the heat. All you need is a small ultra-light rod, a reel, and a few "beetle spins" or other small artificial lures. Put on some worn out tennis shoes and well air conditioned overalls and you're all set.

August 1, 2004, I loaded up ol' Blue with boys and headed for Box's Creek. The boys were all excited when I told them we were going to wade to the water fall. I love trips like this because there is always something to see. Deer, turkey, and other game are always close to water during the hot, dry months of summer and fall. The farther we went the more anxious the boys were to see the water fall. After three hours of hiking, sometimes on slippery rocks, we were all ready to take a break. As we rounded the last bend in the creek, we came to the waterfall. The boys were disappointed to find only a three foot waterfall. I told them to cheer up because this waterfall had some secrets that made it very special.

On each side of the creek, giant old beech, hickory, and oak trees seem to stand guard. The forest canopy makes it difficult for the sunlight to dance with the water, but a few diamonds of light sparkle on the surface. On top of the waterfall a solid, flat rock is perfect for sliding over the edge and into the pool below. A long time ago, an old wagon road crossed the creek here, and it is easy to imagine many picnics happening here. I told the boys that the Indians used these places and they should look around for arrow heads. It wasn't long before Wesley Tucker found two perfect arrowheads. When it came time to go, we made some pictures and everyone was grinning big. They begged me to let them stay a little longer, but it was time to head for home. As we walked back to the truck I told them that there are some unknown places just as special as the ones that are famous.

Wade fishing with today's light weight equipment is very different from the simple cane pole and live bait that I used in the early seventies. Mallard Creek has always been a hot spot for me. The creek is in a canyon for most of the journey to the Sipsey River. The timber along its banks has escaped the power saws and logging trucks, giving the creek a dark, mysterious feeling.

August 2, 1972, I decided to put in at the Beech Tree Hole and wade to Wyer's Bridge. The temperature felt twenty degrees cooler in the canyon than it was on the top. I had just turned the bend above Blue Springs branch when I stopped in my tracks. I could smell cigarette smoke and knew I was not alone. As I looked around, I saw a little man sitting on a log and I recognized him as a friend of my dad. His name was Curt Millwood, and when he saw me he asked, "You lost, boy?" I told him I was not and that I was just fishing. I remembered Dad telling me that Curt had been known to make "moonshine" whiskey, but that he was a good man in spite of his reputation. Curt asked to see my stringer, and I proudly showed him my catch of fat bream. I told him I had a lot more fishing to do and if he would take what I had already caught it would lighten my load. He was pleased to accept the fish, and later we became good friends.

In 1983, I bought the Texaco service station that my dad had owned for the past twenty three years. Curt was a regular customer and was there every morning at 5:00 am. Dad, who was retired, liked to open up early and he always had a table set up with instant coffee, hot water in the pot, and little packets of sugar, and cream. One morning, Mom and Dad had taken a trip to Louisiana, and I opened the station right on time. My first customer was Curt and he told me to make him a cup of coffee. I replied that everything was set up on the table and he could help himself. He said, "Boy, I want you to get me a cup of coffee." I told him that I didn't drink coffee and didn't know how to make it, but he insisted, so to the coffee table I went. I had seen Dad spoon some coffee into those little Styrofoam cups, so I figured eleven or twelve spoonfuls would be enough. I poured hot water in and stirred it. It was so thick; you could have used it to ice a cake. Old Curt had on a greasy John Deere cap and one sip of that thick, black coffee made his cap do a double somersault! He had to admit that I did not know anything about making coffee.

"Tucker's Texaco Station" 1958 --Drawing
by Linda Farris

Chapter Fourteen

....

Big Wheels Keep on Turning

Since July of 1977, a blue Chevy four wheel drive has taken me to many fishing spots that I love so much. Ol' Blue as it is affectionately called is mentioned in the same breath as my name. My boys and I stopped at a local service station recently where there were six or seven old guys sitting on the bench outside. One of them said, "Don Tucker, when are you gonna get you a new truck?" Before I could answer, Gormand Whitehead said that he hoped that I would always go fishing in that truck. He told those fellows that when he saw Ol' Blue headed to the river, he didn't have to worry that his gates would be left open, or his crops would be run over. It gave him great peace of mind, and he also knew it would not be long before Don brought him a mess of fish. Mr. Gorman could not have said anything that would make me feel more proud.

Over the years I have always tried my best to live by the angler's code. My boys have been influenced by it as well. They don't have to be reminded to pick up any trash, keep gates closed, stay out of fields, have the utmost respect for the landowner, and share your bounty.

The boys have asked me several times, how many miles Ol' Blue has on it. I tell them I guess close to half a million miles. The first year I had it, I replaced five different speedometer chains, but I am thankful to say the rest of the truck was of better quality. I ordered Ol' Blue straight from the factory from the Chevy dealer in Fayette, Alabama. The only extras I wanted were heavy duty axles, transmission, transfer case front and rear chunk, and big mirrors on each side to make it look cool. I collected old bottles in the early seventies, and I still love the feel of glass, but I sold my collection of rare bitters bottles to pay for my truck. I paid $5,400.00 for Ol' Blue, and I have never regretted it.

The only change I made to my truck was taking the snow tires off and replacing them with a set of jumbo "mudders." Dad couldn't understand why I would want to take brand new tires off and put more expensive ones on, but I told him I didn't plan to need snow tires in Alabama in July. The sound of those knobby tires is music to my mom. She waits and worries at home if I'm late, until she hears those tires singing, as I come up the highway toward home. All the boys' moms worry, but I think Mom must have it down to a fine art.

I take my responsibility of watching out for snakes, spooks, and boogers very seriously. The first time Miles Henderson went setting out hooks with me, I knew that I had to set an example of what his Mom could expect, or she might send out the National Guard to find us. It was August 2, 2003, when Miles and some of the other boys went with me to set out hooks. Now, I had set out hooks the night before and had left everything in Ol' Blue, ready to go. A box of chicken livers had also been left in it, in the hot, August sun. When we got to the river, the boys unloaded all our gear out of the truck and into the "Titanic", including that rank box of chicken livers. After our hooks were set out, we ate supper at the mouth of the Little River. The boys wanted to do some bank fishing first and Miles wanted to know what bait to use. I told him that if he could hold his breath and put those stinky livers on his hook, he could use them. He baited his hook and then, wiped his hands on his tee shirt. He smelled so bad that we made him ride in the back of the truck on the way home. About midnight we pulled into his driveway and as Miles got out I told him to look there at his mom waiting for him at the door. I said, she sure did love him and he should go up there and give her a big ol' hug for Don Tucker. As that boy greeted his mom with a big hug, she made a face that could sour milk. She yelled, "Don Tucker, what have you done to my son?" I laughed all the way home.

In 1977, Derm Tidwell, Jackie Haley, Tucson Stovall, and myself all bought Chevy four wheel drive pick up trucks, but mine is the only one that has survived. We went fishing, hunting, camping, and courting in those trucks. Tucson changed the look of his truck much more than the rest of us. He worked at a machine shop and made his own blocks so he could raise it up. He then went to Tuscaloosa and bought the biggest tires he could find and then added a big set of roll bars. Not long after decking out his truck he went with Rudell Waters and me to the Sprinkle Hole to set out hooks, fish, and camp out all night. I was the one who actually fished, because Rudell and Tucson just wanted to sit and drink beer. About two o'clock in the morning we ran out of firewood. I finally got them awake and explained the problem. Tucson said, "Don't worry, Tucky Lucky, I'll push that big old dead tree over there down." As he backed his truck up to the tree, I began to get the feeling that this was not a good idea. Tucson locked his hubs in and put the back bumper to the trunk of the tree. Those huge tires started to turn and the tree went to popping. As the big pine slowly started down, the top caught in some other trees that were next to it. All at once, the pine broke about half way up and came springing back on Tucson's truck. Rudell and I had to jump into the river to get out of the way. When the dust had settled, the roll bar had saved Tucson's life, but the tailgate was flattened. Later, Rudell told Tucson to cheer up, we had enough firewood to last us seven winters. I learned a valuable lesson that night. Never wake up a couple of drunks to help you solve a problem.

It is not unusual to have three or more boys go fishing with me. I never turn any of them down, when they ask to go, even though the "Titanic" sinks more often when it is overloaded. Ol' Blue has limited seating in the cab, so the boys like to climb in the boat that is loaded in the back of the truck. We travel the Walker Bottom road to the river, because the traffic is light. It is an old gravel road about four miles long and any fan of the "Dukes of Hazard" can enjoy its' thrills. A mile before you cross the railroad there is a steep little hill that gives them a thrill every time. The boys look forward to it because, if you are sitting in the back and we are going fast enough, you will experience zero gravity for a few fleeting seconds. I tell them that ol' Blue is truly amazing, it can even train astronauts.

A few years ago, Mom and I were coming from the cabin in my old work truck, a 1974 Chevy long wheel base pickup. As we crossed the river in Walker Bottoms, the transmission took out on it. Mom was saying we would have to walk home, but I discovered that it would go in reverse. I told her to watch the side mirror, and I would watch the one on my side, and we would drive home in reverse. As we slowly backed up the old gravel road, Mom was saying she sure did hope no one saw us. In a little while a truck caught up with us and Mom covered her face with her hands and exclaimed, "Oh dear, they will think we're drunk!" I told her not to worry, they probably were saying, those drunks do better at going straight backwards than most sober folks can going forward.

I wish everyone had as many good friends as I do. I'm talking about the kind of friends that will come and pull your truck out after it gets stuck, at two o'clock in the morning, or bring his hundred thousand dollar car hauler into the muddy river bottoms, after I have left my lights on and run the battery down, or put his spare tire on my truck after I have had a flat. One time is good, twice is special, but four times in one month is fantastic. Jacky Haley, Derm Tidwell, and Scot Tucker are very special friends to me.

Best friends are the folks you can count on when trouble finds your door. Every time I go fishing I remember friends who have passed on. It seems to me that I can keep them with me by telling of the good times spent on the water. Their presence in my heart keeps those big wheels turning.

Chapter Fifteen

The Rod Rack

The center of the Angler's chest is open at the top, which allows me to stand my rods and reels upright with the butt end of the rods resting on the top of the compartment that holds my set hooks and throw lines. The rods rest in twenty seven grooves at the top. Front and back rails give the rods a look of springing forth. Like sunlight through a cloud, they stand as if at attention, ready at a moment's notice to supply me with a stringer full of good times. All twenty seven have stories to tell, and fish to brag about.

Five of the rods and reels belonged to my Dad and are now retired, but they still occupy places of honor. Two of his rods were ones he used surf fishing and the one he was using in the post card picture is a Penn Baymaster. The big rod with the giant Pflugar open-face reel is always front and center. This was also Dad's snatching rod. It catches your attention immediately because of its size. It was once a pool cue. Dad tied eyelets, which are big enough to stick my little finger through, and a heavy duty clamp holds the big Pfulgar reel on the rod. The reel has two eyelets on top so the angler can hook up two brass swivel snaps that are attached to his belt. "Snatching" is done below a dam, where the big fish congregate, searching for an easy meal.

Dad used heavy duty braided line on the reel and a two pound lead weight suspended a foot or two below a 16/0 treble hook. To fish with this rig, you simply let the line out until you hit bottom, then snatch the rod up so the tip was pointing to a two o'clock angle. No bait was used on the big treble hooks. Dad said that if a fish swam by in the same county, he'd catch him. He caught some really big fish with this rig; a fifty six pound spoonbill catfish, a sixty nine pound blue catfish, and an eight pound, four ounce small mouth bass, just to name a few. The small mouth bass was caught in the tail and it pulled so hard it felt like a much larger fish.

This type of fishing is illegal now, below most dams, because of the danger of someone hooking into a giant fish and not having enough sense to cut the line. I'm sure the folks who make the fish and game laws in Alabama have saved me from drowning in the Tennessee River, because if a big ol' catfish drug me in, I would have trouble deciding whether to cut off my arm or cut the line.

Eight of the rods standing in the angler's chest are what I call "buddy rods". These rods are really just glorified cane poles. The five ultra-light rods, that I love to wade and float fish with are, on the other hand, high tech works of art. The abuse of constant use, slick rocks, low hanging tree limbs, and fish going ballistic, would be fatal to most rods of lesser quality. Three rods are hard core bass fishing rods, in the sixty dollar range. They are nice, but the four Eagle Claw rods have caught enough fish to feed five or six third world countries, and the cost between the two is quite different.

Uncle Mac Farris once had an experience that perfectly fit the comparison between the high priced rods and the Eagle Claw rods. He was walking down the street in Double Springs, Alabama and as he passed two men standing on the sidewalk one of them called him over. The man pulled a dollar out of his pocket and gave it to Uncle Mac and said, "Mister, I always said, if I ever saw anyone uglier than me, I would give him a dollar." Uncle Mac pulled fifty cents out, handed it to the man and replied, "To be honest neighbor, there ain't but fifty cents difference between us."

At this year's reunion my mom's sister Tava didn't want her ugly old walking stick to be seen in the group picture. She said that she didn't need anything else to make her look eighty years old. However, that walking stick does come in handy sometimes. Not long after the reunion, Aunt Tava heard a noise coming from her carport. She opened the door, turned on the light, and saw a raccoon eating the cat's food. When she raised her cane up toward the raccoon, he put his little paws up to hide his face. I told Aunt Tava that the raccoon was thanking God that she was an eighty year old woman with a stick, and not a rottweiler!

There is one rod that is easily my favorite. I call it "eagle eye Annie" after Andy Griffith's rod on his show. One episode of the "Andy Griffith Show" was written about his famous fish catcher. My old rod has proven time and time again how well it can perform. It is the first rod I ever bought and it would probably be passed over at a yard sale but, this simple rod has caught more fish than all the others combined. Many of my boys know its' power, and always want to fish with it. At one time it had a nice cork handle on it. That is long gone and now the metal butt end is easy to stick into the bank after the line is cast. This old warrior has given friends, family, and myself many wonderful memories of fighting fish, battles won and wonderful food. The biggest large mouth bass I have ever caught was caught with this rod.

On May 2, 1969, my brother David and I were fishing in the early morning on Kelly's lake. The sun was still asleep when we got there, the wind was calm, and the temperature was warm, for early spring. We each had one on the stringer when a huge bass struck my lure. He took line so fast that, if the drag on the reel and rod strength had not been perfect, he would have easily escaped. He jumped only once, but I will forever remember the sight and the feeling it gave me. The big bass put a fight that seemed to last forever, but finally he tired and David got a hold on him and on the stringer he went. He weighed nine pounds and nine ounces and was simply beautiful. Since then "eagle eye Annie" has continued to provide that wonderful feeling that an angler gets from a tug on his line and a bend in his rod.

David liked to fish, but he truly loved speed. Whether it was a juiced up muscle car or a fast motorcycle, he indeed had a need for speed. His street rod, "Twister", is still remembered by drag racing fans in our neck of the woods. David had a fear of growing old and going fast made him feel younger. He was also the most competitive person I have ever known. Everything was a game to be won and while I might intentionally miss a shot in a one on one game of basketball or blow a big lead in dominoes, fishing was different. May 15, 1994, was the last time we fished together.

At the end of May 1994, we were flying back to Alabama from Angel's Camp, California. I had competed and won the frog jumping contest in Fayette, Alabama and the prize was an all expense paid trip for two to the Calavaras County World Frog Jumping Jubilee. On the plane, headed home, we talked about what a wonderful trip we had. So many great people and places that we would not have experienced had it not been for a little old bullfrog, named "Leroy". Less than two weeks later, David was killed in a motorcycle accident coming home from work. His death has left a void in my heart that has not healed. I think of him every day and know that his grandson, Harley, would have filled his heart with joy just like his son Brennan did. Both are red headed mischief makers.

We never realize just what we might miss if we don't have a chance to grow old. David loved life and wanted to live it to the fullest. The last day at the fair grounds, where the frog jumping contest was held, David said he really wanted to try the bungee jump. There was the biggest crane I had ever seen, and folks would climb up, have the cords tied on, and then jump. A giant air bag was positioned below, where the jumper would be let down when he stopped bouncing. It cost forty dollars and when you paid, you were committed, and could not get your money back, even if you changed your mind. I paid for David to jump and told him that if he backed out, every Tucker on earth would hear about it. Climbing that crane was tough work, but he finally got to the top. "You could see all the way to Alabama from up there", David said later. I asked him how it felt to dive out into thin air, and his answer was, "Like a celebration of life."

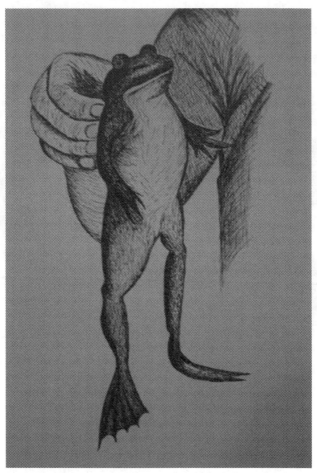

"Leroy" --1992, Alabama State Champion Jumper"
Drawn by Linda Farris

Chapter Sixteen

....

Slick Minnows

Every angler dreams of catching a trophy fish to hang on the wall. My friend, Jerry Poarch, was telling me about a big bass he caught recently. He was fishing in a private pond and was told he had to put the big ones back, so he reluctantly released his eight pound trophy. I told him he could still have it mounted, as he had weighed and measured it, and then when his grandkids asked about that fish on the wall, he could tell them the story of catching it.

My dad's uncle, Murray loved to fish and he was very fond of alcohol. One night Dad gave him a ride home because he had had a few too many and as they started up the steps of his house, Aunt Maggie was standing at the door. She said, "Drunk again". Uncle Murray looked up at her and said," You too, Maggie?" I never saw him take a drink, but he taught me at an early age the importance of lively, big, slick minnows when fishing for "lunkers". He paid me a nickel a dozen for all the slick minnows I could catch.

Town Creek flows through our little community of Eldridge, in the northwest corner of Walker County. This little stream is slick minnow heaven. I first caught them with a hook and line, then I got a couple of rusty old minnow baskets from my brother, David, and business really improved. Before long, Uncle Murray started bringing stringer after stringer of lunkers to Dad's station to show them to everyone. He would just grin when asked what kind of bait he used. Over the years I have caught more than my share of trophy fish, thanks to the slick minnow.

Rusty Whitehead was also a true believer in the power of slick minnows. He loved to set out hooks, and his bait of choice was always the slick minnow. Ol' Rusty would walk a mile up Tucker branch, just to have enough bait. One year Rusty was given a brand new minnow basket as a Christmas gift, and when spring came he put his new basket in the creek to collect bait for our next fishing trip. When we went to check the basket, there was a large cotton mouth snake in it. Every time Rusty tried to open the basket, the snake would strike. Finally, Rusty gave up, cut a big limb off a tree, and beat that new minnow basket as flat as a pancake. He said, "You know, I didn't like that new basket, anyway."

Catching enough bait for setting out hooks is a breeze today, compared to the old days. My friend, Casey Hall, made a couple of minnow baskets for me, and I put them in the deeper holes of the creek. More water means more bait to catch. I really love those big baskets because the small minnow baskets don't work as well in the deeper holes. When the boys bring a friend along they like to volunteer their friend to get the bait out of the bucket. They know there always seems to be a few surprises in my bait buckets and crawfish can always get their attention. Chad Henderson calls them, "slick minnows with pinchers". It seems that some of those big ol' crawdads are so tough that they could grab hold of a fish and throw him on the bank for you.

Kevin Seals is my friend and the plant manager at the lumber treatment plant where I work. One day he was hooking up the "bush hog" to his tractor, and when he looked down a huge cotton mouth snake was between his feet. I asked him later how fast he could run the hundred and his answer was, "a whole lot faster than I thought I could".

Kevin asked me if I could catch that snake, and I told him I could as soon as I could bring one of my big baskets to work. The next day, I put my basket in the edge of the pond, close to the spot where Kevin had seen the big snake, and the following day we went to check it. I knew that minnows would go into the basket to eat the bread I had put into it and the snake would follow them in to get a meal. Sure enough, I had caught the "biggest cotton mouth" I had ever seen. I plugged up the holes in each end of the basket and we loaded it on the truck to show everyone at the office. After we had shown him off and scared all the secretaries, Kevin said he hated to blow a big hole in my basket when he shot the snake. I told him to get his gun ready to shoot, and I would let the snake out. I opened the basket, out he came and I hollered for Kevin to shoot. Now, that old snake was moving pretty fast, but from a distance of five feet, with a shotgun, he should have been dead meat. Kevin missed by, at least two feet, and when I told him to shoot again, he said he only had one shell. (Barney Fife with a shotgun.) We had to run that snake down and kill him with a two by four. I told Kevin he should never brag to me again about being a good shot!

The little branch beside Dad's old service station is a good place to catch slick minnows and where there are minnows there are snakes. One night my mom and I were invited to my sister-in-law's home, which is behind the old station, for one of her fabulous spaghetti suppers.

After supper I decided to check on my minnow baskets. When I pulled up one of the baskets, it had six water snakes in it. I went back in and told Mom and Margaret to get ready for a snake killing. Now, this old woodsman knows the difference between poisonous and nonpoisonous snakes, but I could tell when I brought the big basket out under the light that the girls had their doubts. I armed Margaret with my brother's old 22 rifle, Mom had an old mop handle, and I was ready for battle with my trusty beaver dam rake. I told them to get ready and as I opened the basket, snakes went everywhere. Margaret took aim with the rifle, lowered the gun barrel, and the magazine and every shell in the gun fell out. You would be surprised how fast an eighty six year old woman and a fifty year old fat man can move when properly motivated!

A very productive form of fishing on the Sipsey River is float fishing. June 15, 1982, was a very hot day and my friend, Rex Whitehead, and I were fishing on the Skiff Landing hole. Rex was sitting up front with his feet dangling in the water. As the slick minnows we were fishing with got smaller, the fish we caught got smaller. I caught a small bream and had hooked him too deep so, I pitched him back in the water. A while later the bream came floating up, right between Rex's feet. I told him he better get those stinky feet back in the boat before he poisoned the whole river!

Chapter Seventeen

The Tackle Box

Every angler knows the importance of selecting the right tackle box. Its contents give the angler a wide variety of options with which to fish. Spare hooks, line, sinkers, and corks are as important to those who stay hung up or tangled up as they are to those who actually fish. My tackle box is just a smaller, more portable version of the angler's chest. An even smaller and lighter tackle container is my fishing vest. It is great for wade and float fishing, and it keeps its contents close to this old angler's chest. For bank fishing, a strong tackle box is very important. Plano has been making tackle boxes for years and is the only kind I have ever used. My love for bank fishing down on the Sipsey River makes it important to have a box strong enough to sit on.

My Dad was also a Plano man and after he died I couldn't bring my self to open his tackle box. I finally opened it and a flood of priceless memories came flowing out. The first thing I saw was a pack of Marlboro Lights. Dad had supposedly quit smoking 30 years ago, but we knew he still slipped one now and then. He never smoked in front of Mom or me, and only a very few close friends ever saw him smoke. No one in our family ever confronted him about it, because we all loved him and would never want to embarrass him.

Soon after I bought the Sprinkle Hole property, Dad decided to farm the two fields. The bottom field is eight fine acres of river bottom land. The soil is black and loamy, and so fertile that corn seems to grow while you are looking at it. The hill land is a six acre field of gravelly soil that changes to red clay loam. Early one Saturday morning, Dad loaded up his tractor and was off to plow the fields. We always closed the station at noon on Saturday, and by the time I got there he had about half of the hill field broken up. I told him I would plow some and let him take a break. As he got down from the tractor he stooped down to pull some weed stems from around the right front axle, and when he walked away I looked down and saw his "Bic" lighter lying on the ground. I smiled to myself, put the tractor in gear, and buried his lighter in the soft dirt.

About half way around the field, I noticed that Dad had the door of "ol Blue" open and was going through the glove box. I completed the round, and Dad waved to stop me. He said, "Give me your truck keys, and I'll go to the store for some cold drinks." I told him I wasn't thirsty and before he could reply, I started on my way again. Now, I knew there were no matches or lighters close by, so I took my time making the next round. As I came close to the end of the field, he walked up and said he was thirsty. I told him that Mom had sent a gallon jug of ice water, and it was in the back of the truck. Again, I took off plowing before Dad could say anything. The third time around he walked in front of the tractor and told me that he had tasted that water, and it didn't taste good, so he had poured it out. He insisted that I let him go and get us some cold drinks, before I got over heated. As he drove away

I had a good laugh, because I knew those cold drinks would have a hot companion in the form of a new lighter or matches and a lit cigarette.

Dad's cigarettes in his tackle box reminded me of one of the most unusual baits I ever heard about. Early August, 1979, saw all the creeks and rivers out of their banks because of hurricane Frederick. Even lakes and ponds were full to overflowing and fishing was almost impossible for two weeks. My brother David was anxious to take his young son Bren fishing, so I suggested we go to Curt Millwood's catfish pond. We drove up to Curt's house and David said, "Curt, this boy has never caught a fish." Curt showed us the best place to fish, but after trying red worms and chicken livers, we had no luck. Curt said for us to be patient, and got a bucket of catfish food to help make the fish bite. As he threw handfuls of feed into the pond, the fish came to the top to eat, so I put a cork on Bren's line, about a foot above his hook, but still no luck. Curt looked at David and me and said, "Boys, you are supposed to be the experts." I replied that my tackle box was full of "gollywhopper" baits but these fish would only eat catfish food. Curt's eyes lit up, and then he told Bren to reel in his hook. He took the lead sinker off and the chicken liver came off next. He then took the cigarette from his mouth, cut off the filter, and put the filter on the hook. As soon as Bren tossed it back into the pond, a big catfish was hooked. The fish thought the filter was a brown piece of feed. As we stood there and watched Bren struggle with that fish, we were rewarded by seeing a big grin begin to spread all the way around his head. That wasn't a world record fish, but to Bren it was close to it.

Curt Millwood was in the navy during World War II, and the first battle he was in was on Guadalcanal, in the Pacific. Many times, I had heard Curt say that a good soldier soon learned to adjust and improvise, in order to survive, and that all Americans need to support our troops in uniform and the veterans who laid the foundations of freedom. He was as right as rain, and he showed us his ability to improvise.

May 13, 2000, my friend, Rex Whitehead and I were going to the Tennessee River to fish below the Wilson Dam. On the way up there I asked Rex to stop at one of those "supercenter" type stores. As we walked to the sporting goods section, I told Rex about reading an article in "Field and Stream" that said that a cheese and blood bait was a sure fire catfish lure. We were standing in the check out line when Rex asked me how I was going to keep it on my hook. I looked at all the stuff on the shelves by the cash register, and spotted some panty hose. I asked Rex to get them for me, and he almost had his hand on the package when he realized what it was. He was embarrassed and said, "Don Tucker, I'm not about to pick those things up with all these people watching me."

With a grin, I spotted some balloons and picked them up. Rex asked what I was going to do with those. I told him I would squeeze the blood bait into the balloon; tie a simple clinch knot in the open end. Then, I would put my hook through the balloon to allow the bait to ooze out. When we got to the river and were ready to bait our hooks, Rex said, "Please don't embarrass me by putting a balloon on your hook". I replied that the only thing that would be embarrassed would be the fish, flopping in the bottom of the boat. As soon as my bait hit the bottom, a fine, three pound catfish was tugging on my line. Rex grinned and said, "Well, there is one dumb catfish in this river." Without having to rebait, I quickly put my hook out again. As soon as it hit the bottom, another fish was on the line. I caught five more before Rex said, "All right, Don Tucker, give me one of those balloons and some of that bait." Ever since that trip, I keep a balloon in my tackle box.

My cousin, Kenny Hendrix, from Detroit, Michigan, is a true, diehard fisherman, an ex-Marine, and tough as nails. (His aunts say he's a lot like our Papa Hendrix, who was tough, but quiet and gentle.) Ken suffered a near fatal accident at work, and it took several months of rehabilitation and therapy for him to recover. June 11, 1992, he and his son, Mark, came to Alabama for some much needed rest and relaxation. Kenny's tackle box is big enough to hide a body in, so we offered to carry it down the hill to my brother David's pond. I told him we could lighten it by taking out some of the big lures that he used to fish for muskie, northern pike, and walleye, but he just grinned and said he never knew when he might need them. After two hours of fishing in my leaky ol' twelve foot aluminum boat, Kenny was hurtin' in places he didn't know he had. As we started back up the hill, we again offered to carry his tackle box; but Kenny just grinned and said he could handle it. Later, I told David that I would always carry my tackle box, if I had as much good stuff in it as Ken had in his.

Every Christmas I seem to receive a fishing vest as a gift, and I really love to wear them when I go fishing. The vests are perfect for keeping light tackle close at hand. Pockets of every size keep my tackle separate and prevents a tangled mess. On top of that, they just look "cool" when you wear them. A while back there was a FLW fishing tournament on Smith Lake and the city of Jasper hosted a "meet the pro's" banquet at the community center. Bartley, Eric and I went to the banquet and I wore a "Mossy Oak" shirt, my cool fishing vest, with several patches on it from Stren Fishing Line, Mustad Hooks, Plano Tackleboxes, and the Bass Angler's Society. I topped it all off with a FLW tournament cap that my brother-in-law had given me. We knew we were going to have a fun night, and as we mingled with the crowd, I had nine different kids come up to me and ask for my autograph. As I signed my name for one little boy, Eric grinned and said, "These kids are so blessed to be in the presence of a living legend."

Chapter Eighteen

....

Born to Fish

Confidence and determination are key ingredients to the level of success for any angler. The top professional anglers, who we always see at the top of the leader boards, must know in their hearts that they were "born to fish." Watching them fish on T.V. is relaxing to me, because I love to fish so much. Men like Roland Martin, Jimmy Houston, and Bill Dance must surely have that feeling that they were "born to fish" and win tournaments, but others are born to fish to put food on the table. My Dad was born in 1917, and his family did not have a refrigerator or freezer. Many times, he told of walking five miles to the river, and fishing all night. When morning came the fish caught were brought home for the family to enjoy. I can testify that a breakfast of fresh caught catfish, eggs, gravy, and biscuits is a wonderful thing.

As a young man, my dad had walked almost everywhere he went, and I guess all that walking is probably what turned Dad toward truck driving. He was as surely born to drive a truck, as I was born to fish.

Dad's first job was hauling coal from the small mines north of Eldridge. His truck was a three ton vehicle that had to be loaded with a shovel. He then drove it to the railroad track side ramp, in Eldridge, and shoveled the coal onto a freight car. Dad's pay scale was fifteen cents a ton. That is 15 cents a ton for loading and unloading three tons of coal!

I once asked Dad why, on all the old black and white pictures, taken before 1950, no one was smiling. He said, "If you had to work like we did back then, you wouldn't feel like smiling either". It is easy for me to understand why he loved hunting and fishing so much. It gave him a break from the every day trials of making a living.

Mom and Dad were together for sixty two years. One day, not long ago, Mom and I were strolling through the grocery store, and I asked her what was on her first grocery bill. She told me that Dad had gone to J.A. Kelly general store, in Eldridge, and came home with flour, baking soda, lard, an ax, (to cut kindling for the wood cook stove) and a new butcher knife. How she cooked a meal with these things, I don't know, but she is a great cook, and she still uses that butcher knife. If I had a nickel for every tomato she has cut with it, I would be a millionaire. Mom says that even though times were tough, they were never hungry or ever felt like they were poor.

As times improved and transportation got better, Dad began to head for the Tennessee River to fish. He became successful fishing for catfish, bass, and Jack salmon, but it was crappie fishing he loved most. Dad always found time every spring to crappie fish, and I can vividly remember being awakened at three o'clock in the morning, so we could be on the water early. Some times we would rent a cabin and stay the whole weekend. It was there on the Tennessee River that I learned the fine art of crappie fishing and with each trip I became more confident and determined to be as good as my Dad. Dad caught several three pound crappie in his lifetime, the largest being three pounds, fourteen ounces. In April of 1964, I caught my first three pound crappie out of Mr. Elvin Engle's pond, just north of Eldridge.

August 27, 1990, Dad and I fished the "bend hole" at my "sprinkle hole" property. The slick minnows in my baskets were our bait as we fished at Tucker branch, and the crappie were really tearing those minnows up. For a while it was just like old times, and each fish on the stringer made us grin even bigger. By the time we ran out of bait, we had ten crappie; each one weighing one pound or better. June 13, 1991, we again found the crappie biting, and in no time at all, we had put twelve big ones on the stringer. This was Dad's last crappie fishing trip.

Most folks buy land in order to make money from it by farming or cutting the timber, but when I bought the thirty acres that border the Sipsey River, in 1989, I was investing in the good memories of the past and the hope of making many more in the future. The "sprinkle hole" place gave me two priceless fishing trips with my dad that will be cherished for the rest of my life, and that same property was the site of Dad's last dove hunt on September 27, 1997. Dad was a great shot, and I asked him once how he learned to shoot so well. He said, "Well son, it means a whole lot more to you if you are planning on having something to eat."

A favorite place to dove hunt has always been J.T. Tidwell's farm on "Barn Creek". September 18, 1993, was opening day for dove season in Alabama, and dove hunting is as much a fall tradition in the south as college football. Having all the equipment ready and properly organized is as important as the actual hunt: the guns must be cleaned and in working order, a shell box or a five gallon bucket is a more comfortable seating choice than the ground, a portable radio is necessary for listening to the game, and you need a cooler full of cold drinks and snacks to help you enjoy the day. I also bring a couple of plastic bags full of ice to keep the drinks cold and preserve the field dressed birds. When we arrived, J.T. was sitting under a big pine tree behind his barn. The tree had been struck by lightning and was dead, and it's limbs were perfect for the doves to light on before flying to the ground to feed. J.T. had already killed seven or eight doves, so I went to work cleaning those birds and discarding the wings, heads, and feathers off to the side. As we visited with J.T., his six year old grandson, Derrick, came walking up and asked his "Paw Paw" how many birds he had killed. J.T. pointed toward the little pile of wings, heads, and feathers, and said he had seven or eight. After Derrick had walked over and looked at those feathers, he exclaimed, "Damn, Paw Paw, I believe you are using too big a shot!" After we recovered from laughing, I told J.T. that my folks had always said I was born to fish, but I believe Derrick was born to hunt.

Chapter Nineteen

....

Forced to Work

Optimism and the anticipation of a tug on his line, keeps an
angler casting that lure. I have never met a pessimistic fisherman,
they simply don't exist. Every time I run my set hooks, I just know
That one will produce a fish big enough to brag about. My mom is the
ultimate optimist and I saw a good example of her optimism recently
while we were standing in line at the funeral home. One of our town's
older citizen's was lying in state and just about everyone from Eldridge
was present to pay their respects. As we stood in line, Wesley Tucker
walked up and asked, "Ms. Iva, what do you want people to say about
you when you are lying in there?" Without missing a beat, and with
a smile on her face, Mom said, "I hope they say, "I think she's still
moving".

I have tried to be an optimist at work, but my heart is not in it,
even though I know I am blessed to have a job, and it be no more than
fourteen miles from home. When anyone asks me about my job, I tell

them that they pay me more than I'm worth, but not enough to brag about.

After completing an application for work at the Southeast Wood Treatment Plant in Nauvoo, Alabama, in June of 1994, I was sent to the plants manager's office. When I walked into his office, I was surprised to see an old hunting and fishing buddy. Kevin Seals had been a regular customer at the service station for years, but he had moved north and we had lost contact with him, for about three years. We talked about old times and then Kevin asked me when I could start work. I told him, the sooner the better, because I was anxious to pay off the loan I had for the thirty six acres of land I had recently bought. When I got home, Dad asked me about the benefits, and I told him that I had good insurance and after a year I would get a week's paid vacation. Dad said, "Son, you've been on vacation for the last eleven years, here at the station".

Before long a fishing trip was planned with my boss man and on August 30, 1994, Kevin Seals, Ken and Karen Tate, (who also work at Southeast Wood) and myself went to the mouth of the Little River, which borders my "Walker Bottoms" place. They brought a very large cooler with them, and about four hours later we had a full stringer of fish and I had three drunks on my hands. If you have seen a drunk person fall down on a flat surface, you can imagine my problem trying to get three drunks up a slick river bank. A few days later my boss asked when we could go fishing again and I told him to wait a while, because I needed to rest up from our last adventure. That fishing trip was thirteen years ago, and, thankfully, I haven't had to tote anymore drunks up the river bank.

This country's criminal justice system has been criticized for its failure to rehabilitate its repeat offenders, but it actually convinced my boss that drinking and driving don't mix. He was traveling through south Alabama, and was stopped and arrested for being over the limit. After he was booked he was taken to another room and told to strip his clothes off. Then, the biggest black man he had ever seen came in with a canister that had a sprayer attached to it. Kevin said the big man with the sprayer only spoke two words, but they were chilling enough to change a man's habits. Those words were, "Bend over".

I have never been drunk nor smoked a cigarette and don't really understand how anyone can afford liquor and cigarettes. It takes every dime I earn to just get by. My twelve foot, aluminum boat, the "Titanic", only cost fifty dollars, but there's probably a thousand dollars worth of welding repairs on it. I have to work hard just to keep it sea worthy, because being the sentimental type is expensive. My boys all understand that if you want to fish and not sink, you better be wiling to work up a sweat bailing water. It always amazes me that the same boys who beg to get out of mowing the lawn, on a riding lawn mower, to go fishing, will tote, pull, and drag the "Titanic" over every shoal and log jam, up and down the river. Their dads can't believe that they are willing to work so hard to fish, but I tell them that good things happen to those willing to work.

Professional anglers are constantly looking for ways to improve their position on the leader board. I was watching TV one day as the top ranked pros were practicing for a big tournament. One angler was asked about his chances of winning and he calmly started up his Stihl chainsaw and said he could cut his way to even the most isolated places. He was clever to find a way into unfished waters, but he must think it's a shame to be forced to work in order to win, because fishing is just too much fun.

Summertime fishing in Alabama can get really hot. Water levels in lakes, ponds and streams begin to drop and this forces many anglers to wait for cooler temperatures and better water conditions. Wade fishing in a creek or river is my way to beat the heat, but this form of fishing is not for the faint of heart. Snakes are a constant hazard, and ticks, chiggers, and "skeeters"can turn a cool way to fish into a fight for survival. Being the optimistic fisherman that I am, I prefer to think of only the pleasant things, and the best thing about wade fishing in September, is Mom's homemade, muscadine jelly.

Every year I begin to scan the vines that hang over the river, for the plump, purple grapes. September 6, 1999, Chad Henderson, Tyson Lawrence, and myself found a good, full vine a little way up from the mouth of Mallard creek. The boys would throw a stick up to hit the vine and it would rain muscadines for five minutes. We caught a stringer full of fish and a bucket full of muscadines. I told the boys what my friend Doug Howell, had to say about Mom's jelly. He said, "It's so good it's got to be illegal, but it's worth doing time for."

I always try to have one or more fishing buddies along to help gather up the muscadines, because I had learned a few years ago that this job could be hard work, and could also be hazardous to your health. That day I found a good vine just below the "cyclone bend" in Mr. Wyman Jones' bottoms. I used an oak tree root that weighed about three pounds, to throw into the vines and knock the grapes off. The river current swung in, under the vines, and the knee deep, sandy, white bottom gave way to deep water, close to the bank. If muscadines floated, this would not have been a problem, but since they don't, I had to be ready to scoop them up before they rolled into the deep water.

The vine hung heavy with fruit, and my five gallon bucket was quickly filling up. I had tossed the oak root time after time and always kept my eye on it, to see where it would land, but the first time I failed to watch it, I had to pay. The blunt end came crashing down on the button at the top of my baseball cap. I didn't remember anything for a little while, but as the cobwebs cleared, I had to laugh. Almost getting killed is serious business, but getting killed picking muscadines is ridiculous. When I got home, I told Mom that being forced to work for jelly had almost retired me from the business of living!

Chapter Twenty

....

Reel Peace

Recreational fishing is a billion dollar business, and fishing tournaments offer the opportunity to catch a dream to a few. However, for most that enter the tournaments, the difference between winning and loosing is only a few ounces. Fishing has so many angles that it's easy to understand why the flashiest fishermen catch the most television time.

I recently read that fishing license sales were declining in Alabama because of a lack of places to go fishing. I don't agree with this theory, but think a lot of folks think that you have to own a sixteen foot bass boat, with a 150 horsepower motor, and ten rods and reels that cost more money than you can shake a cane pole at to go fishing. While those things allow the angler to fish like a pro, they are not all there is to fishing.

Going fishing early in the morning puts me in a peaceful state of mind. It doesn't matter if it's on a glass smooth farm pond, a foggy morning below Smith Lake Dam, or running my set hooks on the Sipsey River. Early morning brings peace to your soul, whether you are using a cane pole or a sixty dollar rod. I like to get to the water before daylight, so I can fish that special time just before the birds awake and begin to sing.

August 3, 1996, Kevin Eads, Casey Farris, and I arrived at the Curt Hubbert bridge to run my set hooks. As we walked up the river bank, to where the "Titanic" was docked, the fog was close to the ground, with only the top of the old Indian mound visible. When we reached the boat, the morning came alive with sound. Owls were calling to each other, song birds were saying "good morning", and the squirrels were getting busy. Up river, the splash of a fish on a line also got our attention. When we had loaded into the boat, I turned on the trolling motor and we headed to the nearest bouncing cane pole. Kevin turned to me and said, "This sure is a "cool" way to fish". I asked him if he knew who invented "cool". He wanted to know who, and I replied, "God invented "cool". Genesis 3:8 states that God walked through the garden "in the cool of the day", and since the Bible is the inspired word of God, then He invented "cool". Casey added, "And besides that, you couldn't call the Devil "cool", in that tacky red suit".

That fishing trip was eleven years ago, and those boys are all grown up now. Casey is now teaching school in Houston, Texas, and he and his wife Tammy have a young son and a little girl, and they both look like their daddy. Kevin served two tours of duty in Iraq as a U.S. Marine, and is now married and a restaurant owner in Mobile. I always told "my boys" that when they got all skinned up, sliding down the river bank or walking through a briar thicket, that it will only improve their looks. Trading "hide" for good looks surely did pay off for these two.

May 27, 2006, Chad Henderson, Wesley Tucker, Bradley Prescott, and I went to my "lower forty" place to do some late night gigging. This trip was special for two reasons. The fish we caught were big enough to brag about, and the crew I had was a good mix of old pros, Chad and Wesley, with Bradley, who was anxious to fish with the big boys. We caught twelve that night, including two thirty pound gars. After taking their pictures, I told the boys that these were the size fish you could expect to catch in heaven. Bradley asked, "Don, just what do you think we'll do in heaven?" I said, "Well I think we'll get to fish, eat ice cream that won't make you fat, and fly around without the fear of heights. Maybe we'll get to snowboard over the clouds, feel love and have no fear of anything." Bradley sighed and said, "Good. I figured we would just sit around, being quiet, while God preached to us for all eternity."

Fall of the year means fishing and college football. My peace and happiness during this time depends largely on how many games the Crimson Tide wins. I am perfectly calm, as long as the "tide" continues to roll, but when the team struggles; my vocabulary seems to go to hell. I guess I'm just too full of Alabama pride. Every Saturday, my mom sends up a heartfelt prayer for Alabama's team to win, so peace and happiness can reign in our home.

October 29, 2005, Mom suggested that I carry my radio on my fishing trip to the mouth of Mallard Creek. The big game wasn't on television, so I loaded up for a fishing trip, down on the Sipsey River. The weather was great and so was the team. After hollering myself hoarse and eating all the hotdogs and cake, Mom had packed for me, I returned home blissfully happy. Mom asked how many fish I had caught, I told her that I must have caught the only fish in the river that were deaf and suicidal.

Some people seem to think if you go fishing and fail to catch anything, it's a wasted trip, however, and I consider my "fishless" trips a blessed opportunity to learn something new. Over the years I have become a devoted bird watcher and catching a glimpse of a rare or exotic bird makes my day. Mom has also fallen in love with the feathered friends that visit our bird feeders. She says they give her a happy feeling of peace by being so happy to have food to eat.

One morning as I was getting ready for work, she asked me to do something about the squirrels, because they were destroying her bird feeders. I went to the gun safe and pulled out my "Daisy Red Rider" BB gun, Dad had given me, for Christmas, when I was eight years old. When I came home that afternoon, I noticed the BB gun was out on the carport; so I knew she had used it. I asked her about her squirrel hunt, and she complained that the gun wasn't any good. She said that when she saw the squirrels on the feeders, she had walked within three feet of them to shoot, but when she pulled the trigger, the BB's had rolled out the end of the gun. After having a good laugh, and explaining how you load a BB gun, I told her maybe we should just buy new bird feeders, more often.

I have always tried to teach "my boys" to look for those unexpected things that seem to make every trip special. July 17, 2004, Eric and Alex Aultman, Miles Henderson and I set out hooks at the "skiff landing" on the Sipsey River. As we slowly drove around the fields to reach our destination, Eric said, "We always have good luck when we go fishing in these old foggy bottoms." I told Eric that a fisherman's luck is a wet ass and a hungry gut and he replied, "Yes I know, but we are not allowed to say words like that." I told him that he was right and that he should never do or say anything that would shame his Mama. Then I said, "Let me rephrase that quote. Say, we went fishing in the foggy bottoms and left them with a stringer full of fish and a soggy bottom. "Sometimes the fishing can be so good, that the angler fails to see the things that make the experience truly memorable.

August 7, 1998, Scot Henderson, Scot's son Chad, Tyson Lawrence, and I were on a float fishing trip, down the Sipsey River. The stretch of river we were on was especially rough, with log jams and shoals to cross. Even though the going was tough, the fish were biting with almost every cast. As we rounded the bend, the waterfall came into view and it is a beautiful sight as it tumbles straight down a cliff and splashes into the river. The boys were so busy catching fish that they hardly noticed the falls. I told Scott that if the boys wanted to catch a big one, they needed to be on the big flat rock where the waterfall hit the river and cast along the bank. When Chad and Tyson stepped under the falls to make their cast, the cold water hit them and made them notice that this was a very special place. We let them go swimming and enjoy the waterfall to their hearts delight. They begged to stay longer, but time was slipping away, and as we floated on down the river I told them they looked like two blue popsicles.

Anglers the world over are always looking for that flash of color that only a fighting fish, tail walking above the surface of the water, at the end of their line, can give. July 9, 2001, Casey Farris, Chad Henderson, and I were pond fishing when a flash of color made fishing insignificant. A rainbow formed over us, the colors so intense, that it filled our very souls. Later that week I asked my friend, Scott Tucker, if he had seen the rainbow. He said, "I not only saw it, I know where it came to the ground." I reminded him of the old myth about a pot of gold being found under the end of a rainbow. Scott replied, "Well, I'm not superstitious but just knowing that all I have to do to get it is, dig up my driveway, gives me peace of mind."

"Wade fishermen" --Alex and Wesley

Chapter Twenty-One

The Angler's Chest

Standing **three feet three inches** tall, five feet long, and two feet wide, the angler's chest is the center of my fishing world. It is made of Sand Mountain, Alabama, walnut that has been seasoned and sanded 'til the strength and character of the wood reveals its true beauty. Each drawer contains a different type of fishing equipment, hooks, sinkers, floats, line, reels, flies, lures, and tackle box. The double doors at the bottom reveal my set hooks and throw lines. The center section displays the rod rack. This is not just a place to store my fishing gear, but it is actually a treasure chest of good times spent in the pursuit of happiness, and the promise of more to be had in the future. Many people spend their entire lives searching for their "treasure chest", without realizing that it was right in front of them the whole time.

I became a member of the Alabama Treasure Forest Association in 1989, because the two hundred and sixty three acres I own in Fayette and Walker counties are indeed treasures to me. The scenic beauty and wonderful good times they provide make them true treasure chests. Americans are blessed with ponds, lakes, creeks, and rivers, full of good times just waiting to be enjoyed. We have fields of flowers and grain, gardens and forests, seashores and mountains, plains, deserts, and canyons and we should be out enjoying their beauty and grandeur more and worrying about the six o'clock news less.

My uncle, Kirg Hendrix, knew where his treasure was, but he had a problem. She lived in Carbon Hill, and he lived seven miles away in Eldridge. Transportation was difficult to come by in the 1930's, so he would jump on a train going in that direction, get off in Carbon Hill, and walk to Kat's house to "court" her. When it was time to go he had to hop on another train, jump off when it reached Eldridge, and walk two miles home. This worked fine until he hopped on a freight train and discovered when it reached Eldridge that it was going too fast for him to jump. When it finally slowed down, he was in Tupelo, Mississippi. Every time he told that story, he would smile and say that a man would do anything for love.

Uncle "Bud" Farris tells a story about working at his dad's sawmill. Across the field and up the Byler Road a piece from the sawmill was the house where his treasure, Oveta Hendrix, lived. Bud's job at the mill was to set the blocks as the logs were cut into lumber. After several mistakes and miss-cut boards, Mr. Frank, stopped the saw and walked over to Bud. He said, "Son, I know you think your heart's treasure is up there in that house, but today my mind is on sawmilling, and I want your mind on my business."

March 15, 2003, Chase O'Mary, Heath Tidwell, Stephen "Big Cat"Colburn and I went "sucker gigging" on Barn Creek. When we got to the creek, Chase told us to wait while he put on chest waders. I said, "Son I've never had anyone wear those heavy waders before." Chase replied that nothing could be worse than freezing to death in that cold creek. Before long we found the fish shoaling and our stringers began to fill up. The first three shoals were gravel, and Chase was making it fine, but the fourth was solid rock bottom and when he stepped on that slick rock, down he went. Instantly, those chest waders filled with water. Unable to get up, with so much water holding him down, he lay there with a surprised look on his face. I pulled him out, took hold of his heels and when I raised his feet, the water washed his hat off. Later, I suggested to Chase that there was something worse than freezing in that cold creek water. You could drown and freeze to death! Those treasured waders had left him all wet.

The expression, "home is where the heart is", certainly applied to my Dad, even though he traveled many miles, driving a truck, and loved it, he really loved home. In the 1970's Dad drove for a company that built boats for bass fishing, and he delivered boats all across the Southeast. On one trip to Louisiana, his truck broke down and was going to be out of service for a week. His boss told him to get a hotel room and wait there while his truck was being fixed, but Dad told him he would be coming home, because he would not miss Thanksgiving at home. On hearing that, the boss, who was an old hunting and fishing buddy, said he would fly Dad home in his new airplane. It was much smaller than Dad had envisioned and when he got on board he found very little room to stretch his legs. Dad was amazed that the little Piper two-seater lifted off with such ease, but once they leveled off he enjoyed looking down at the fields and forests below. His boss said, It looks like we are just sitting still, doesn't it?" Dad agreed and said, "Yeah, but, if you have trouble, don't expect me to get out and push". My Dad was a treasure with his wonderful sense of humor and big smile. He was a man of great strength and character, and we were all proud of him.

Dad died in the room where the angler's chest stands. Mom's mother, Mama Hendrix, also died in this room. She was a lady of great strength and character and she raised a wonderful family of ten children. Some might think this room would be a sad place, but the love and happiness these two people gave us make it a special place. Their memory will never die as long as the angler's chest and this old angler continue to tell the stories that bring joy to the heart and a smile to our faces.